Jim's Book!!

R
BETWEEN

CENTRAL BUREAU
FOR EDUCATIONAL VISITS & EXCHANGES

LONDON EDINBURGH BELFAST

Every effort has been made to ensure the accuracy
of the information contained in **A Year Between**,
but the Central Bureau for Educational Visits &
Exchanges cannot accept responsibility for any
errors which may exist, or for changes made after
publication. All rights reserved throughout the
world. No part of this publication may be
reproduced, stored in a retrieval system, or
transmitted, in any form or by any means,
electronic, mechanical or otherwise, without the
prior permission in writing of the publishers.

First edition

© Central Bureau for Educational Visits &
Exchanges 1991

ISBN 0 900087 88 9

Distributed worldwide by the Central Bureau for
Educational Visits & Exchanges, Seymour Mews
House, Seymour Mews, London W1H 9PE
℃ 071-486 5101
Fax 071-935 5741

Distributed to the book trade by Kuperard
(London) Ltd, 30 Cliff Road, London NW1 9AG
℃ 071-284 0512
Fax 071-284 0519

Cover illustration: Barton Stabler/Image Bank

A Year Between was compiled and edited by the
Print, Marketing & IT Unit, Central Bureau for
Educational Visits & Exchanges, London

Typographic imaging and print production by the
Print, Marketing & IT Unit, Central Bureau for
Educational Visits & Exchanges, London

Printed and bound in Britain by BPCC Hazells

CONTENTS

Section VII

COMMUNITY & SOCIAL SERVICE

Section VIII

YOUTH WORK/CHILDCARE

Section IX

CHRISTIAN SERVICE

Section X

STUDY OPTIONS

Section XI

TRAVEL ADVICE

INDEX & REPORT FORM

USING THIS GUIDE

Section I Practical Options, provides an introduction to taking time out, offers advice and information to those thinking of taking a year between, a personal checklist to evaluate potential, a discussion of the key elements of being a volunteer, plus a section on further resources. The introduction covers the pros and cons of a year between and examines the attitudes of all those involved. The personal experiences of students and employers is recounted; further first-hand accounts are under Section II and the individual placement sections. The personal checklist offers a programmed series of questions to enable all potential particpants to evaluate their current assumptions. There is no easy path in coming to a decision as to whether or not to take a year out, but this checklist should help a reasoned decision to be more easily arrived at. A period of voluntary service requires commitment; it can be emotionally draining and physically exhausting, but the spiritual rewards can be high. Potential volunteers will find some vital questions here for consideration. To complete this section there are details of organisations who can offer further advice, careers counselling, short courses or other opportunities for those taking a year between. Sources for further reference on paid and voluntary work opportunities, sponsorships, further study and grants, plus details of useful guidebooks for expeditioneers and travellers are also included.

Section II Years of Experience, is a series of contributions from the major organisations in the year between field, giving examples of how they feel their projects benefit both participants and host community.

The opportunities themselves are detailed under separate sections covering the type of placement available. Each section begins with a general introduction including comments from those who took the year between option, after which organisations are listed alphabetically, each entry giving a brief profile of the organisation and full details on the projects available:

Training/work experience Opportunities to work in industry, administration, tourism and commerce, where participants can earn a wage and gain valuable work experience.

Discovery/leadership Exploration, expeditions, adventure programmes and short service commissions in the armed forces offer opportunities for travel and self-development.

Conservation/land use Opportunities to work in the great outdoors, including agriculture, horticulture and other work on farms, kibbutzim and moshavim. Opportunities for practical contributions to the environment through conservation projects are also detailed.

Teaching/instructing Teaching English as a foreign language, or acting a teacher's aide at schools in Britain and abroad.

Community & social service Projects caring for people in need, such as offering assistance to people with a physical disability, working with the homeless, or helping out in a community for those with mental handicaps.

Youth work/childcare A range of opportunities to work on projects for children and young adults, some of whom may be disabled or disadvantaged. This section also includes information on au pair work.

Christian service Community, social, evangelical and ecumenical projects based in Britain and abroad. Applicants should have a Christian commitment or at least be thinking seriously about their faith.

Study options Ideas on short courses and language study, plus opportunities to spend a term or an academic year at a school abroad.

KEY Information on the organisations offering the opportunities in the placement sections has been provided in a set format to aid selection and provide easy comparison:

 Name and address of organisation

 Telephone number

Countries/areas Details of where placements are made, or the countries in which participants may be placed. In some cases the placement destination depends on the projects in operation in a particular year, or is at the discretion of the organisation.

Profile A general description of the aims and activities of each organisation, together with its status (whether commercial, private, non-profitmaking or charitable) and the main fields of activity

Opportunities Details of the type of opportunity available, with a general description of what participants will be expected to do. Where possible, we have given details of the number of placements the organisation makes each year.

Requirements Age limits for applicants: some organisations cater for school leavers, others will only accept applications from postgraduates. Details are also given of the personal qualities, skills, experience and qualifications that participants will require. Any language requirements and nationality restrictions are specified. Where applications from people with a handicap are considered, this is indicated as follows:

B vision impaired
D hearing impaired
PH physically handicapped.

Duration Length of the placement, including any minimum and maximum periods. **A Year Between** covers, in general, placements lasting from 3-12 months. Shorter-term opportunities open to those having a year between are covered by the companion guide **Working Holidays**.

Terms and conditions covers details of any costs to participants, hours of work, salary or pocket money provided, holiday entitlement, type of accommodation, and whether travel and insurance costs are covered

Briefing Details of any orientation course held prior to departure or any debriefing at the end of placement, plus information on any on-the-job training or supervision, additional training and language courses

When to apply Applications and requests for information should be made to the organisations direct, and not via the Central Bureau. Early application is always advisable, as many projects may be full to capacity well in advance of the closing date. When writing to any organisation a stamped addressed envelope should be enclosed, or, in the case of an organisation overseas, an addressed envelope and two International Reply Coupons, available from post offices.

The final section of this guide gives practical advice and information on travel and related issues, for example medical requirements, insurance, passports, visas, coping in an emergency, and contains an index and report form. Up-to-date reports on organisations placing those on a year between enable us to improve the accuracy and standard of information in this guide. At the end of your year between we would appreciate the completion and return of the report form to enable us to monitor the work of the various agencies and employers, and to enable us to record your experiences.

PRACTICAL
OPTIONS

A YEAR BETWEEN

A year between - up to 12 months between school and higher education, school and work, or higher education and a career - is a rare chance to stand back, assess where your education has brought you so far, and seize the freedom offered to undertake something completely different, possibly on the other side of the world. It gives you the opportunity to develop skills, become more self-reliant and achieve an understanding of your own strengths and weaknesses. But before you make any final decision, it is worth weighing up the pros and cons and asking yourself why you want to take a year between.

Is it simply because you want to see the world? Or do you want to become more mature, responsible, open minded or tolerant? Do you want to earn some money and develop skills before starting academic life? Do you feel that the self-discipline imposed by higher education is something you can't yet cope with? Or are you attempting to delay the moment when you start your working life, concerned that you are unprepared?

Discuss your ideas with family and friends, teachers and careers advisers. How will a year out help or hinder your aspirations to higher education or a career? You may want a break from what you see as a conveyor belt education system, or from the pressure of exams. But does this mean you will end up having to explain away a gaping hole in your *cv* to potential employers? The idea of being a year older than your peers when you get into higher education may appeal, but then again, you may find it more difficult to settle back down to study. Do you wonder if you should grab what may be your last chance to broaden your horizons and experience new cultures, or would you feel more secure getting your education over and done with in one go and embarking upon a career?

There are no wholly right or wrong answers, but as the final decision is down to you, it is vital to be honest with yourself. If you do decide to take time out the process of examining your reasons and considering the advantages and disadvantages will help you to plan and organise how you intend to fill your year. And when an admissions tutor or future employer asks you about it, you're more likely to have a well thought-out response.

Deferred entry If you intend to go on to higher education after taking a year out you can apply to your chosen institution either before taking your A levels (or equivalent) requesting that the entry be deferred, or during your year out once you know your exam results. Some institutions have a preference for deferred entry; others would rather make unconditional offers based on exam results. Deferred entry is a sensible idea if you are likely to be on the other side of the world, and therefore unavailable for interview, during your year between. However, higher education institutions have a difficult task allocating hundreds of places conditional on exam results, and because of the numbers involved some faculties can offer only a few deferred places. It is best to contact the admissions tutor to discuss possibilities; in some cases the prospectus will provide details on deferred entry.

Higher education institutions certainly do not appreciate applicants who are offered a conditional place and then wait until the last minute (usually once they have their results) before asking for their entry to be deferred. They are also wary of applicants who defer for a year then decide not to take up the place. Whilst time to reconsider is obviously of benefit to the applicant, late decisions such as these may deprive other candidates of a place and affect the institution's ability to fill target quotas. The best advice if you opt to defer is to state your intentions as soon as possible, and if you do change your mind let the institution know at the earliest opportunity.

After graduating Many students consider taking a break once they have their degree qualification under their belt. You may feel you have earned time to relax after exam pressures and see this point in time as your last opportunity to do something different before settling down. Or you may be unsure of your career plans and see a year out as a chance to learn about yourself and the type of work that suits you. However, you should be very wary of going off on a year between without having made plans for what you will do on your return. It might be a good idea to finish off your year out with a short course to develop new skills, in which case you should try to arange it beforehand. Take advantage of employers' visits during the milk round to gauge their reactions and opinions about your taking a year out. Or, if you have no fixed career plan, get advice from the careers service to see what type of work would interest you, and consider what personal skills and aptitudes you would like to test out in your year between. At this stage it is important to have at least some plans for the future; it would be a big mistake to assume that everything will just fall effortlessly into place once your year out is over.

Attitudes to a year between Apart from the possible problems of logistics posed by deferred entry, most higher education institutions have no objection to students taking time off before embarking on a course of study, provided it is spent in a worthwhile way. For courses such as sciences or engineering a year spent gaining relevant industrial experience is viewed very favourably. However, mathematics is often quoted as being a subject requiring continuity of study, and some tutors may view a year's interruption as detrimental. A year between

may also be discouraged before long courses such as medicine or architecture. It is best to discuss your plans with the admissions tutor, or at interview.

We asked institutions whether students who had taken a year between had problems settling down again to study. Of those who had available information, most stated that they had few or no problems, or that any problems were soon overcome. Things you learn at school don't get forgotten that quickly, but if you're concerned about losing touch, then exercise the grey matter by reading relevant books and periodicals, and do stay in touch with current affairs.

Many institutions agreed that students who had taken a year out before their course showed more maturity and better defined career aims. Some even went so far as to say they were more likely be better achievers academically. The following quotes are just two examples of the overwhelmingly positive feedback we received:

The consensus in this university is that students who come to us after a year out are more mature, better able to organise their time and better motivated. Senior Assistant Registrar, University of Reading

Most deferred entry students are generally more motivated than the 18 year old straight from school. Senior Admissions Officer, South Bank Polytechnic

As far as employers are concerned, again they are more likely to react positively to a year out if they feel the time has been spent in a relevant and worthwhile way, such as on an industrial placement or working to develop skills and experience. They are perhaps less enthusiastic about a year out taken after higher education - they may have suspicions that you found it difficult to get a job, that you lack drive and ambition, or that you have lost the momentum of your years of study. You must be able to convince them that you have not spent your time drifting or doing nothing, and that your experiences have left you a more mature and capable person. If you can present clear and logical reasons for having taken a year out, and explain how you have benefited from the experience, they will find it easier to view you as a potential employee:

When assessing a candidate's application we always look at it on an individual basis. Travel or a year out will not in itself be a positive factor. However, if the candidate can demonstrate that they have learnt and developed as a result of the experience then this would be seen as a strength.
National Recruitment Manager, Ernst & Young Chartered Accountants

We see any kind of work experience as a plus point in an application, and obviously a year out, if spent constructively, is viewed in a positive light.
Graduate Recruitment Coordinator, Harrods Limited

Planning and preparation It is most important to plan your year between well ahead of time. Eighteen months may seem rather a long time in advance, but if you start to make plans in the lower sixth, or before the final year of your degree course, you will have a wider range of options open to you and plenty of time to consider them before exams creep up on you. If you leave it late because of indecision or because exam results weren't as expected you may find that many schemes have no places left.

Think about your reasons for taking a year out, and on the basis of these, plan what sort of things you want to do. If you want to see the world consider whether you want to travel independently, work or volunteer overseas, or join an expedition. Will you need to raise money to pay travel costs? You may have to spend some time trying to earn it or raising sponsorship. Many people follow a period of voluntary service by a period of paid work; this gives a good mix of experiences, projects and countries, and helps to balance limited finances. Would you rather gain work experience where you can use your A level qualifications or see how a particular type of employment will suit you? Many of the opportunities in the **Training/Work Experience** section are for those with good results in science-based subjects, but there are also placements for students of any subject.

Remember that future employers will want to know how your year was spent, and what you gained from it overall. If you spend a whole year doing nothing in particular or working in a mundane job then potential employers are unlikely to be convinced by your ability to assume the responsibilities and take the initiatives involved in working for them. Plan things well in advance instead of in a last-minute rush and your year between has a better chance of being worthwhile.

Do it yourself! One thing we would like to stress is the importance of doing things for yourself. It can be very easy to rely on your parents to do all the dirty work for you, especially if you feel you've got other, more pressing commitments. However, one of the main principles behind taking a year between is to become more independent. This is incorporated into the philosophies of many placement agencies, who are looking primarily for applicants who can demonstrate self-reliance and maturity. So it is worth starting right now, at the planning stage. If you can't rely on your own capabilities to plan a year between, how will you cope when you are far from home, or in an alien environment, or when crucial decisions have to be made? Of course you should seek advice from parents or teachers, and discuss your ideas with them, but try to ensure that the majority of the initiatives and planning comes from you, and that you're the one making the final decision - this is all part of the challenge!

When writing to any organisation you should mention where you found out about them (for example, in **A Year Between**). Introduce yourself, explain briefly when you will be available to take up a placement, why you are interested in their opportunities in particular, and in what way you feel you are a suitable candidate. Enclose a large stamped addressed envelope, especially if you are writing to a voluntary or charitable organisation. Don't go into too much detail at this initial stage; in all probability they will send you an application form where you can enthuse at length about your qualifications, interests, experience and suitability for the placement. Keep a copy of all your correspondence and application forms, as these will probably be referred to during interviews - or may even get lost in the post. Make sure you apply well within any deadlines; some placements have an element of first come, first served, so the earlier you apply, the better.

Depending on the organisation, candidates are selected firstly from the information given in their application forms, then on the basis of their performance at interview or on a selection weekend. Such weekends usually consist of a series of challenges set to test aspects such as decision-making skills, ability to work in a team, physical stamina, motivation, determination and commitment, and may include items like assault courses, outdoor pursuits and group discussions. Before attending an interview or selection weekend spend some time thinking over your reasons for applying to this particular organisation; read through any literature they have supplied; consider how your skills, qualifications, experience and personality fit you for a placement and what you hope to gain in the long term.

If you are selected, you may also be asked to attend further training. These training sessions are valuable, not just in preparing you for the work you will be doing, but also by allowing you to meet your future colleagues, find out more about the organisation itself, and discuss the project in detail. You owe it to yourself, the organisation and the people with whom you will be working to ensure that you are well-informed before beginning the placement, so do your best to find out as much as you can. Talk to people who have previously worked with the organisation, and who can give you information based on personal experience. Read any field, project or expedition reports that are available.

If you are going on a placement abroad, read up about the country. The relevant embassy or tourist office may be able to provide some information, but it is also worth investing in a good guidebook, such as those published by Lonely Planet or in the Rough Guides series. The organisation arranging your placement should be able to provide help and advice on visas, work permits, medical precautions, travel and insurance, but it is down to you to make sure that these aspects are settled well in advance to avoid any last-minute panics. Remember that in some cases medical protection can take the form of a course of injections over several weeks, so allow plenty of time.

Finally, try to prepare yourself mentally for the experience. You will be meeting new people, attempting new tasks, perhaps finding out about new cultures. Expect the unexpected, and keep an open mind.

Fundraising Many organisations arranging placements or expeditions overseas require you not only to pay your return fare, but also to contribute towards administration and organisation costs. This figure may end up in the thousands, so you will need to think of ways to raise funds. Getting a job which will earn you enough money to pay the whole amount would be ideal, but it may take you a while to save up the sum required.

If you want to try tapping alternative sources then start by publicising yourself. If you make enough of a splash locally people will have heard of you when it comes to asking them to give their support. Tell your local newspaper and radio station all about your plans - where you will be going and the work you will be doing. Make it sound as exciting and as worthwhile as possible. Keep them informed throughout your fundraising campaign - it will encourage others to contribute when they see you have a target to reach. If you can, offer to send regular press bulletins once you've begun your placement. Keep copies of any press articles featuring your project to use during your campaign.

Publicise yourself at school, at university, at church, at your parents' social club or work. The bigger the network, the more likely you are to find someone who can help, if not financially, then with advice, further contacts or equipment. Organise sponsored events - the more imaginative they are, the more likely they are to hit the headlines, but don't attempt anything too dangerous or time-consuming! Try harnessing your creative talents to design jewellery, paintings or T-shirts; grow house-plants; make cakes; become a pavement artist... Organise fundraising events such as jumble sales or barn dances. Whatever you do, remember to explain the point of the exercise, and tell people what the proceeds are going towards.

Find out if there are any grants available from your local authority or from businesses and trusts. The reference library should have a copy of the *Directory of Grant-Making Trusts*. Published by the Charities Aid Foundation, this directory lists voluntary grant-making bodies in England and Wales covering all fields of voluntary activities. Also, try contacting local companies; they may be interested in the publicity afforded by a goodwill gesture to a local young person.

When writing to organisations such as businesses or trusts, remember that a personal letter is likely to get more attention than a photocopied circular. Keep it fairly brief: tell them about your project, ask for their support, and explain how the project is relevant to that particular organisation - for example, will it enhance the company's green or caring image; does it fit in with the aims of the trust? In return for support, you can offer to use their products overseas, write articles or give presentations describing your experiences when you return, or publicise their contribution in the local newspaper (enclose any cuttings featuring your project).

Raising money is very hard work, but if you summon all your reserves of imagination and determination your target can be achieved. You can generally count on help and advice from the organisation who will be placing you; they will already have plenty of fund-raising experience. Lots of other people have managed to fund themselves - so can you!

Other people's experiences If you're dithering about making the final decision to take a year between, how to plan it, what to do, when, and where to get the finance, then have a read through the following accounts, collected from young people we contacted in the course of preparing this guidebook.

Jacci Wilkie, who went on an expedition to Indonesia in summer 1991 with Trekforce Expeditions says that for her taking a year out was of tremendous benefit:

After leaving school I went straight to university without really having spent time thinking about what I wanted to do. When I realised I'd embarked on the wrong course and was fairly miserable about the whole situation, I decided to take control of my life.

I worked on a night shift stacking shelves at Tesco for seven months so that I could pay for my intended trip to Indonesia. Although I sincerely hope never to have to do this job ever again I am glad of the experience. It's increased an awareness in me that not

*everybody's as fortunate as I am.
I also feel I possess a stronger ability to
empathise with and understand other
people's problems as I was mixing with folks
I ordinarily wouldn't come into much
contact with.*

*The whole year, including the expedition,
was a massive learning process for me. I
learned many things about myself, but more
importantly I came to the realisation that
life is really very, very short and is too
valuable to waste. We should seize our
opportunities while we have the energy to
do so, and make the most of everything we
do.*

Lera Miles also took time out in 1991. She
didn't venture as far afield as Jacci, but she
used the time she had available to test out
many different opportunities:

*My year out didn't really start until March.
Before that I stayed in my home town
frantically composing letters to various
organisations offering my services in
exchange for board and lodging.
I made the most of my time by learning to
type and doing some voluntary work locally.
I had not planned to take a year out at all,
but once I had inadvertently entered into
one, I was determined to try plenty of
things.*

*I spent time as a Voluntary Assistant
Warden at a bird sanctuary, helping with
the lambing on a friend's hillfarm, working
as a childcare assistant at a seaside holiday
home, volunteering at the Monkey
Sanctuary in Cornwall and on a children's
camp in Dumfriesshire.*

*I returned to Scotland with a friend to
finish my year with a youth hostelling trip.
Taking a year out has given me some much
needed confidence, some new practical skills
(decorating, axing wood, improved bareback
riding, tea-making, preparation of monkey
food...), social skills, a good cv, new friends*

*and a sprinkling of self knowledge. I now
know for sure that I'd much rather work
with adults or animals than with children.
I also know that I'm capable of doing a much
wider range of jobs than I'd thought. I've
been converted - I would recommend a year
out to any school-leaver.*

Tim Smyth, currently a student at Reading
University, spent six months in Israel working
as a volunteer for the Church's Ministry Amongst
the Jews, a placement which was cut short by the
outbreak of war in the Gulf:

*I was sometimes working nine consecutive
days hard labouring, but the work was
character building and strengthened my
faith. I was given much opportunity to
travel and took it ... I have grown
immeasurably, spiritually and mentally. I
find it easier to talk to minority races in
this country as I know how they feel.*

*I was in Israel during the whole part of the
Gulf Crisis and was only evacuated after
three hours' notice, two days before the war
began. This tested me and my family to the
limit and taught me a great deal about God,
myself, my family and friends... Imagine
being prepared to stay in a country, away
from your family, during a war. In Israel
this meant preparing a sealed room,
collecting supplies, receiving gas masks and
feeling what an entire country feels and
fears. Then to be suddenly evacuated is a
tremendous shock, with all the feelings of
betrayal of the Israeli friends you've left
behind.*

*I can honestly say that the six months I
spent in the Israeli culture weren't enough.
I think I learnt so much about the way I am
and how I react that has only gone to help
me in the way I study. I am more eager and
keen to learn than if I'd gone to university
straight from school, plus the added benefit
of being a year older than my counterparts.
One problem however is that I've forgotten
how to do calculus at the moment...!*

Fiona Hatchell considers that deciding to take a year out in 1990 was one of the most important decisions she's ever made. Looking back she feels that the year changed her attitudes, expectations and perspectives on life:

I spent seven weeks working as a volunteer in an outdoor centre, then worked in an office for four months to raise some money. From January to April I worked as a physical science and maths teacher at a secondary school in Malawi. Teaching at a school with just one other expatriate taught me volumes about the African way of life and living alone in this different environment taught me much about myself and the peculiarities of our Western life. The remaining four months I spent with the British Schools Exploring Society on an expedition in Svalbard, an archipelago just 700 miles from the North Pole.

My year out was entirely self-funded and I consider this as important as the places and people I visited. Had I not had to work hard to raise the money the experiences would not have been quite as satisfying.

Henry Morris worked for Shell Research Ltd for 11 months during 1990-91, where he spent most of his placement working on a feasibility study into the automated inspection of recycled oil drums:

This was meaningful and relevant work to Shell, not a spurious exercise, and was valuable experience for someone about to start a degree in Engineering and Management.

I felt that there was an element of luck about student placements. How repetitive or interesting the work was depended on which department the student joined. I had my own project, and to a large extent was my own boss. Other students spent more of their time working as assistants to senior workers or carrying out routine tasks.

However, it must be stressed that all placements are as interesting/stimulating as you want them to be.

All in all, I think my year was successful. I became a member of the PFUE organisation and through them I was introduced to the Young Engineer for Britain competition, where I reached my regional final and won my age group. The speech to 150 people at the Manchester Museum of Science and Technology at the end of the year must be preparation for any public speaking I will do as an engineer!

Chris Collins spent her year out in 1989 working as a Community Service Volunteer and as a voluntary helper at Churchtown Farm Education Centre where she cared for people with disabilities and organised outdoor pursuits. She is now doing a course in occupational therapy, and feels her experiences have helped her considerably:

Taking a year out was one of the best things I've done. I learnt a lot about myself, other people, and life in general. I grew up a lot in that year. I feel it made a great difference to the way I've coped on my course. If I had started training straight from school I wouldn't have got this far.

Jo Barron took her year out after graduating, and worked for three months during 1991 on a placement with Health Projects Abroad in Tanzania. She was involved in two projects: helping to supply a district hospital with a water and drainage system, and building a medical dispensary.

I didn't make a conscious decision to have a year off after graduating, but now, in retrospect, I am really pleased that I did. I had always been interested in Africa and was keen to get first hand experience of life in a rural developing country, although I never really thought it would be possible. The selection process was quite tough and involved a weekend in the Peak District with tasks ranging from orienteering and an assault course to group discussions and an interview.

Twelve volunteers were then chosen and we were informed of the decision within a week. From start to finish HPA were very friendly, efficient and organised - they kept in touch by letter before the project and organised a training weekend in February which really helped to prepare us for going away from home and living in rural Africa.

The Project Leader in Tanzania had researched and organised everything for our arrival, so that we could start working straight away. The experience was definitely beneficial: working in a team with people that I didn't really know before, working with African villagers and getting first-hand experience of life in a developing country. I saw the problems and way of life in rural Africa and came back with a greater awareness and self-confidence than I had three months earlier.

What next? As you will have gathered from these accounts, after spending a constructive year out your outlook and attitudes are liable to have changed somewhat. You may have had to learn how to cope in difficult situations, how to get along with people from a wide range of backgrounds, how to stand up and talk to a group of complete strangers, how to handle responsibility and make quick decisions. You will probably have come out of the experience a more mature and confident person, and you may also find that academic or working life is a bit tame compared to the challenges that you have faced, especially if your year has been spent abroad, on an expedition, serving the community, conserving the environment or doing work you felt was particularly valuable.

It is understandable if you feel a bit unsettled when you first return. If the challenges you face now don't seem so crucial they are still important ones, and the experiences of the past year will probably help you to meet them. If you are anxious not to lose the momentum and enthusiasm you have built up over the year, then look around for other projects you can help with in your spare time or during vacations. The organisation that placed you may arrange briefings for returners, who can thus share experiences, evaluate the work they've done, keep in touch, even plan new projects together. You may also be able to help them with fundraising, public awareness or briefing meetings for new recruits. We too would like you to share your experiences with us by filling in the report form at the back of this book. Completed forms help us to improve the information and advice we offer, and help us to help you share your experiences with others.

Above all, enjoy your year out.

CHECKLIST

This checklist is for those who from the outset have known they are destined for a year between; for those who haven't a clue what to do at the end of their sixth form or degree course; for those with some idea of what a year out would achieve, but are still firmly on the fence; for those who are determined to slog on with their formal education, come what may; for those who have over a year to carefully plan and prepare for a year between; and for those, who either through lack of forethought and preparation or through indifferent exam results are having to face a last-minute crisis. In short, for all for whom the considerations of a year between are vital. There is no easy path to coming to a decision as to whether to take a year out or not; what this section aims to do is to force self-analysis, cover most of the pros, cons and options, and in so doing allow individuals to arrive at their own reasoned decision.

For those who have always planned to take a year between, this programmed series of questions should radically evaluate your current assumptions:

Have you really made the right decision in taking a year out? Have you been totally honest in your motives? Is what you have chosen to do really the right project for you and your future area of study? Wouldn't something more relevant/totally different be more valuable in terms of educational content/personal development?

Those undecided as to whether a year between will really be of benefit should read of others' experiences in the *Introduction* and *Years of Experience* sections first, then follow through with this section. The questions here should then evaluate individual potential and sharpen your focus. The year between is a time to try out new experiences and test your independence; if you are uncommitted to a year between then these personal areas probably need closer examination:

What is the longest period you have been away from home on your own? How much do you rely on your tutors, parents and friends for support? How well thought-through is your future area of study or eventual career? Has your education to date really tested you? Do you know the extent of your physical and mental limits?

If you are against even considering a year between carefully read this section first:

Why are you in such a hurry to get on with the next stage of formal education? Have you really got a thirst for knowledge or are you simply looking to get away from parental ties as soon as possible? How wide are your educational horizons? Can you hold a decent conversation in anything other

than your chosen subjects and your
immediate environment?

For those with little time left and who are
now having to face a year between with little
advance preparation, don't panic. Yes, many
of the opportunities on offer will have already
gone to those better organised. Yes, with some
forethought you probably would have got a
lot more out of a year between. But no, all is
not lost, and much can be salvaged, even at a
very late stage. Read through this section
carefully, check your options, make a shortlist
of what appeals to you, what opportunities
really will be of value and are still open to
you, and don't be rushed into choosing/
accepting the first opportunity on offer.

For & against

You have decided to take a year between
Check the *For* boxes below which have
formed part of your decision. If you have
additional reasons, list them. In the *Against*
section check those boxes that you agree with.
On balance, is taking a year out still a valid
option? If so, proceed. If not, exactly what has
tipped the balance against your original
decision? Carefully re-examine your initial
decision, examine how you arrived at the
secondary decision, then re-read the
Introduction section. Then start again here.

You are undecided about taking a year out
You should have read the *Introduction* section;
if not, read it now. Then go through the *For*
and *Against* lists, checking those options you
agree with.

*Do you come to a positive conclusion?
Have you any reasons of your own to add to
either list?* Continue on to the next part.

Still on the fence? Read the *Years of
Experience* section. You should then be on one
side of the fence or the other. Depending on
which side, follow through the choices here
before going on to the next section.

Positive that a year out is not for you?
Talk it through with friends, tutors and
parents; you may be right.

You don't feel a year between is for you
Go down the *Against* list, checking all the
options you agree with. If you have an
additional case to make, list those reasons.
Then go through the *For* list, checking the
options you are willing to consider. Now do
you want to re-evaluate your decision for
discounting the idea of a year between? If
not, read the *Years of Experience* section. If
you are still convinced then a year out is not
for you, then you are probably right. If there
is even an element of doubt, carry on!

For

- ☐ Opportunity to broaden horizons
- ☐ A break from years of continuous education
- ☐ Time to evaluate options
- ☐ Opportunity for independence
- ☐ Time to earn some real money
- ☐ Rare chance to travel at length
- ☐ Opportunity to give rather than take
- ☐ Time for self-development
- ☐ Opportunity to widen contacts with other people
- ☐ Time to evaluate career course chosen
- ☐ Opportunity to try something new
- ☐ Will improve chances on degree course
- ☐ Time to examine other cultures and lifestyles
- ☐ University/family are in favour of deferred entry
- ☑ Other reasons (list below)

Against

- ☐ It will be difficult to return to formal education
- ☐ Out of step with friends not taking a year out
- ☐ University/family against deferred entry
- ☐ Difficult to give up home comforts
- ☐ Course of study long enough without an extra year
- ☐ Not yet ready to grasp opportunity for independence
- ☐ Can't think of a positive alternative to current plans
- ☐ Offered a suitable job now
- ☐ Appears as an unexplainable blank on the *cv*
- ☐ May not be available for college/job interviews
- ☐ Not yet mature enough
- ☑ Other reasons (list below)

Options

Look at the list below and select the one option that you feel offers the most value in your terms for taking a year between:

- ☐ Travelling overseas, discovering the way of life in other countries, evaluating other cultures

- ☐ Working, doing almost anything to earn money, to finance future studies and the opportunity to travel, or to buy that longed-for cd player or new clothes

- ☐ Acquiring work experience/training related to the future areas of study/career, possibly through graduate sponsorship

- ☐ Undertaking something seemingly unrelated to past/future education patterns, but something quite selfless like a community or social service project

- ☐ Doing something possibly quite self-centred, a personal development programme for example

- ☐ Continuing education under your own steam, reading as much as you can about your future subject, learning a new language, finding yourself through philosophy, maybe

Let's analyse your choice.

☑ You opted for work experience or training

Why? The year between is a time to experiment, to make use of an element of freedom you may never have again. Why do you want to tie yourself closely to what you are going to be doing in the near future anyway? Up to 40% of the job opportunities open to graduates are for those of any discipline. What will give you the edge in a job application over a similarly qualified colleague is your personality and your wide-ranging experience. Your potential employer will want to know whether you can get on with people, work as a team, communicate well. Will you be able to take positive decisions then carry them out? Do you know anything about the wider world of work, or are you only familiar with the corridors of *academia*? What you have actually achieved beyond academic qualification will make you stand out from scores of other applicants, and the opportunities for such achievement may only be available to you in those precious twelve months of a year between.

☑ You opted for a year of travel

Fine, but how much of another way of life will you be discovering? You speak the language, have a background to their culture? If you have to finance at least part of your travels by working, how much character-building experience are you gaining washing dishes in some international hotel? Will some future employer misconstrue your travels as simply a skive as you bum around the beaches of the Mediterranean? Maybe you will write the definitive travel guide, discover a tribe who have never seen an American Express card, but unless your travels are well structured, apart from contributing to the ills of irresponsible tourism you will gain little more worthwhile than a tan on your jaunts. Yes, plan in a period of travel during your year between, but don't let it become the be all and end all of your programme.

☑ You need the money and will do almost anything legal to get it
Fine, this entrepreneurial streak will impress academics and employers alike? What did you do to earn the money? And more importantly, what did you do with it then? You may have achieved little beyond informing the world at large of your self-centred nature. And the relevance of labouring on a building site to your future study/career? Some positive benefit if it is civil engineering or architecture, practical materials handling is always useful, but wouldn't that time have been better spent developing more of your personal and technical skills through building an orphanage in an underdeveloped country, for example?

☑ You opted for a period of adventure to develop your personal qualities
A period of testing and self-development is no bad thing in the year between, but make it part of the scheme of things. Relate it to future environmental studies or a science-based career, for example. Make sure there are other goals in sight, or it will turn out as apurely selfish exercise. You may come out of it as a true leader, but then again you may have gone into it rather smug in the first place. You're not planning to be a politician are you? Be careful that this course of action doesn't give the wrong signals of your intentions and limit your options later on.

☑ A period spent acquiring skills in the community
A period of personal growth and maturity? You saw yourself helping others less fortunate than yourself? A little too altruistic, perhaps? Have you read the section *Volunteering*? Careful you are not justifying a period in a far-flung country, with elements of travel and adventure combined with conscience-salving community work.

☑ A period of study related to the future or something different
After something like thirteen years of continuous formal education you want more? Or even more if you've just completed higher education. Sooner or later your'e going out there to get a job. You'll need more than just academic qualifications; isn't this the time to broaden your educational horizons? If you are committed to further study, explore beyond your own subjects.

Having made your initial choice and then read the comments above, do you want to revalue your options? At this stage we are simplifying things by only examining one option at a time; a year between may very well consist of two or more complementary but distinctly different projects. Having re-evaluated your first choice and either having stuck with it or gone for a second choice, check your option below. If you have come to the conclusion that a year between is not for you then it might still be worthwhile looking at the personal experiences throughout this guide. The writers of these accounts are the sort of people you will be competing against on your degree course and in the interview room. You should think carefully about acquiring the fully rounded education that they possess. Your future employer will be asking serious questions if you haven't.

☐ Travelling overseas
On its own this is probably one of the most expensive options, particularly in relation to the perceived benefits. However, relatives,

family friends and parents' business networks can all be used to help you find places to stay. They may also be able to help you find temporary jobs to help you pay your way. Check the statements below that you agree with, then see on balance whether you are still committed to this option:

- [ ] Probably the only time in my life I'll have this length of time to travel
- [ ] The cost, in time and money, is too high
- [ ] My foreign language ability will improve tremendously
- [ ] Travel broadens the mind
- [ ] Not very good at coping in foreign situations, a poor linguist at best
- [ ] The experience will mature me and help me cope on my own
- [ ] Only ever been on package holidays, unsure whether I could handle this
- [ ] The resourcefulness and independent attitude will look good on the cv
- [ ] Not very good at meeting people, coping with new situations
- [ ] Months of travel could look self-indulgent to a future employer

Although you may want a flexible itinerary, some forward planning is essential. Passports, visas, work permits, residence permits, inoculations, vaccinations, medical precautions, insurance requirements - the basic checklist is seemingly endless. See *Section XII* for further information, but be prepared for considerable work on your own behalf. The *Resources* section, pages 25-30 also has useful contacts and publication for further advice and information

[ ] **Earning money**

There are a thousand and one ways of doing this, but care must be taken in order that there are rewards other than financial. For real benefits to be gained the work must either be related to future study/career, or the value of doing something completely different is intrinsic in the activity. For example, work on a building site or on the shop floor can give you experience of life and of work conditions that you might otherwise never face. Even fairly routine jobs in the travel and tourism fields can be of direct educational benefit where foreign language fluency, for example, can be utilised and improved. Certain elements of the business world, such as marketing, can be explored by those with a flair for people contact. In the right context, and for a defined period of time only, sales jobs in publishing, financial services and the domestic installation markets, such as double glazing, central heating or insulation, could be constructive. Much of the readily available work is seasonal, and you need to think carefully about the periods of possible inactivity. Tackled in the right way, even a series of labouring jobs could contribute much to a degree course in the university of life. Is this still the option for you? See whether you are still committed by checking the statements below that you agree with:

- [ ] The money will come in useful for holidays and at university
- [ ] Bit hard going, working for a living; I've just left school
- [ ] I've had enough of education, let's see the real world
- [ ] All my friends are earning now
- [ ] The experience looks good on the cv
- [ ] I'm not sure what relevance grape picking has to my studies/career
- [ ] I can be independent, leave home
- [ ] I'd spend all the money I'll earn, so what's the point
- [ ] The company may give me a permanent job later
- [ ] The company offers me a permanent job now. What do I do?
- [ ] It'll be hard to give up a wage for a student grant
- [ ] My parents are well-off so I don't need to earn the money

☐ **Acquiring work experience**

You may feel the most important factor in taking this option is its relevance to the future course or career. However, the elements of work offered to you as a school leaver or recent graduate may be quite different from that of a qualified postholder. A high percentage of administration work may be involved, and some of it fairly basic. Make this a positive element; it is useful to get experience of all areas of a particular business or service. The networking available will provide employable skills, a vast amount of information, and useful contacts for the future. It may be just the beginning of work on a project that can continue through study and into vacations. Allow yourself therefore the widest options in acquiring knowledge and developing skills that the company can offer. Check the positive statements below so that you're sure this is the option for you:

☐ The work will help me relate better to my course/future career

☐ It will give me the option to see if this is the career for me

☐ It will help me gain sponsorship

☐ I'll become more mature/responsible

☐ All my friends are on holiday while I'm still working

☐ I'll be independent, show my parents what I'm capable of

☐ The company I work for could offer me a job later

☐ It'll make me realise I'd be wasted going on to higher education

☐ I'm not getting wide enough experience of life/other work

☐ **Community or social work projects**

It is sometimes difficult to separate out the demands and differences of a voluntary placement as opposed to a straightforward paid job. In the section *Volunteering* the exact nature of the commitments that voluntary service entails are discussed; the section also acts as a check as to whether this is the option for you. In itself community involvement is satisfying; in the wider context the opportunities to learn specific skills, to work with a wide variety of people, from different backgrounds, nations and creeds, and to give something to others can contribute greatly to the experience of a year between. There are few openings that can offer the wide range of emotions, challenges, demands and rewards that a period of voluntary service does.

☐ **The study option**

The obvious reason for taking a further course of study is to prepare for the next step, whether it be a degree course or a job. The options available, and the reasons for taking them, go far beyond this. A short course could provide a taster of what a degree course entails, and go some way to making up your mind if you're currently wavering. You could use the time to develop your international outlook, either in language study or by acquiring work experience in another country. The oncoming of the Single European Market throws up all sorts of pressing reasons for acquiring a European or international dimension to your skills. The study option in the year between may also give you the opportunity to acquire keyboarding and other computer skills, test out some vocational options, particularly if your degree course is not immediately vocational in nature, or to continue with a subject you may have had to relinquish in order to concentrate on A levels, for example. However, you should ensure that a short course does not deflect you from your chosen path, nor involve you in the heavy burden of financing your own study. Check these statements:

☐ A study course will be expensive

☐ It'll show my study commitment

☐ It will only be part-time; what do I do with the remaining time?

☐ I'll be adding practical educational skills to my cv

☐ Offers little personal development

VOLUNTEERING

The motivations for voluntary service in a year between may be many and mixed, but whatever they are, potential volunteers must be clear, positive and honest with themselves about the reasons for volunteering:

Do you feel voluntary service will give you experience and improve career prospects? Are you running away from facing unemployment/employment/personal problems? Have you a political conviction or commitment to the struggle of disadvantaged people? Have you felt a call from God? Why are you in a position to volunteer?

Considering the importance of the answer, the question of why one is volunteering is often passed over by volunteer and sending agency alike. As a volunteer you may find difficulty in answering, and there may not be a clear-cut answer, but the process of examining the reasons for even thinking about volunteering is a vital one. For those considering undertaking a project in the Third World, their understanding of why those countries are underdeveloped needs careful examination:

Why are there people in need who have to rely on other people's voluntary actions? How do the people of such countries come to be so poor, badly house and underfed, and how can the expertise and investment of the advanced nations help?

Why are you particularly considering volunteering overseas? Is going abroad more exciting? Are you heading for warmer climates?

Although it may not initially be so obvious, the UK has extremes of wealth and poverty, bad housing, illiteracy, high unemployment and an immigrant population which is discriminated against on many levels; working to overcome these problems and their causes is a more than worthwhile challenge.

One thing is clear; time spent in voluntary service is far too valuable to waste. For such an investment of time and energy it is essential that there is a clear understanding of what volunteers expect and what is expected of them.

Voluntary service involves commitment. Projects are essentially mutually rewarding and beneficial; both volunteer and co-worker are expected to be enriched by the experience of working on a common task and to have contributed positively, even if fractionally to the betterment of mankind. Increased understanding of the economic interdependence of the more developed countries and those in the process of development, many of them still below even the lowest poverty line, has led to a reappraisal of the role of volunteers and the relationship to those whom they aim to serve. However to argue that such benefit as accrues from volunteer involvement comes in terms of personal experience for the volunteers is to ignore the vital importance of personal contacts for the growth of mutual understanding and the transmission of skills. In this greater mutual understanding lies the best hope for a real improvement in human happiness worldwide; and the witness of returned volunteers in their own community is or should be a leaven, without which mutual understanding will be increasingly replaced by self-interest and protectionism.

Nor should potential volunteers be confused by the term *voluntary service*. There is no real distinction between paid and voluntary work, nor between work and service. Useful volunteer projects spring from the needs and the initiatives of people at the grassroots, projects in which volunteers help those people construct their self-development. At its best, volunteer contribution, however skilled or technical, is quite different from professional work, being based as it is on the principles of democracy and equality instead of profit.

Which agency? The volunteer-sending agencies will ask volunteers about their background, competence, views and intentions; volunteers have an equal right to ask the agencies about theirs, and they owe it to themselves, the organisation and most importantly to the people they will be working with to ensure that they are well informed. They should talk to representatives, ask to see field reports, and meet returned volunteers who will provide information based on personal experience. The volunteer's personal motivation should not be too much at odds with the general aims of the selected sending agency.

When a potential agency has been identified - be it commercial, governmental, religious of technical in orientation - the volunteer should request further information on its background and philosophy, details of aims and objectives, its scale of operation, the type of enterprise, how it is run, and its support system both in the UK and overseas. Some agencies recruit volunteers on behalf of organisations overseas and so will not themselves be in control of the project volunteers will be working on. The agency should be honest enough to provide prospective volunteers with details of the problems to be encountered, the projects that failed and the basic dilemmas still unresolved after years of activity, as well as their successes. Agencies operating in the Third World should offer their views on underdevelopment and some guidance for the volunteer. The volunteer will be anxious to be selected, but should remember that selection is a two-way process; as much caution should be shown to the agency as they will show to the volunteer.

Which country? Many agencies take the view that volunteers should be prepared to serve where they are needed, their own choice of country being of secondary importance. If they have a specific preference potential volunteers should state this when applying and give their reasons. Questions they should ask regarding the proposed country include its location, climate, and historical and current political situation:

Where in the world is the country? Could you cope with the heat, the dust, the .mosquitoes, the lack of basic facilities? Could you come to terms with the practices and the customs of the host community? Are the priorities of the government of the country the same as those of the majority of the people? If not, why not, and what as a volunteer can you or will you do?

Work assignments Volunteers should ask key questions of their proposed work assignment, for example:

Why was the project chosen to work on? How does it relate to local needs? Who set it up and finances it? What do the duties entail? Who would you report to? How are the decisions reached? Why does the project need the skills of a volunteer? Whose interests will your presence promote? How interested is the recruiting agency in the work you will be doing?

If the project is well-established volunteers should be shown the field reports and debriefing records of previous volunteers. If the project has been successful, they could ask why the agency has not by now trained a local person to fill the post, and in any case, volunteers should check carefully that by going they are not putting a local person out of a job.

Personal qualities Prospective volunteers should take careful note of the personal qualities requested in each agency's entry. In addition, before applying, they should ask themselves some fairly serious, self-searching questions:

Do I get on with people? Am I prepared to learn from the community I will work in? Can I work as part of a team? Can I cope with isolation? What do I hope to gain? How can I bridge the gap between what the project will expect of me and what I am? Could I learn the language?

Qualifications, however impressive, are useless without the right personal qualities. Volunteers must above all be able to communicate, be sensitive, patient, resourceful, psychologically and physically robust and with a good sense of humour. They must want to learn and to make friends.

Terms Many agencies will provide accommodation, board, travel, insurance and some sort of remuneration. Some additionally provide allowances and paid holidays. It should be clearly ascertained how the volunteer is to be paid and by whom, how social security rights are affected and details of insurance provision:

Under what scheme and for what eventualities are you insured? Who will be concerned should you fall ill or have an accident? Where are the nearest medical facilities?

The prospective volunteer should also enquire about job security; volunteers may find themselves doing a completely different job from the one expected, or no work at all, and they will need to know who they can turn to in such an event. They should be clearly informed of the project and what is expected of them. The political climate in some countries is not always stable, and volunteers should establish what security provisions and support they can count on in the case of political or social conflict. It should also be established what happens if, in exceptional circumstances, the volunteer has to leave the project early.

Briefing Some preparation is obviously needed, and it is in the volunteer's interest to request adequate preparation before setting out. Any volunteer-sending agency with a sense of responsibility will make time and find funds for proper training; not all training should be done before leaving, but should be a continuing process carried out at intervals throughout the period of service and include some preparation for the return home. The period of orientation should be long enough to allow the volunteer to take in and digest the information. Volunteers may be living and working in a society where much will be strange and different, and the training is basically to help them understand and cope; they may wish to question the explanations provided for the differences:

Does the training present underdevelopment as something which only occurs in other parts of the world or does it take up questions of poverty and inequality in our own society? What arrangements are there to meet other volunteers and discuss and evaluate their context in the development of the community?

Language is vital if the volunteer is to make contact with ordinary people, and even in countries where English is an official language only a small proportion of the population will speak it; the agency should provide at least basic language instruction. Volunteers should receive up-to-date and relevant technical advice and be made aware of the social and human effects of any technology introduced.

Application Before applying for any project prospective volunteers should check carefully that what they have to offer matches up to the agency's requirements. Applications should be accompanied by a statement of what the prospective volunteer wants to do and why, and a *curriculum vitae*. There may be a lengthy period between acceptance and actual assignment, especially if the project is overseas, and early application is advised.

RESOURCES

Career Analysts 90 Gloucester Place, London W1H 4BL ☏ 071-935 5452 is a professional firm set up to help people of all ages discover the education, training and career opportunities best suited to their needs. Consultants are psychologists who combine expert assessment of aptitudes, interests and personality test results with a personal counselling approach to help each applicant plan their career and make the best possible educational and career choices.

Careers and Occupational Information Centre Room W1108, Moorfoot, Sheffield S1 4PQ ☏ Sheffield (0702) 594563/4/9 or 5 Kirk Loan, Corstorphine, Edinburgh EH12 7HD ☏ 031-334 9821 produces a range of publications, videos and materials dealing with careers, education and training.

Cavendish Educational Consultants 22 Hills Road, Cambridge CB2 1JP ☏ Cambridge (0223) 69483 offer a wide range of services including advice on courses for those taking a year between, re-take courses, educational testing, vacation courses and Oxbridge entrance. Produce an annual *Gap Year Book* giving details of courses and ideas for a year between, available free.

Central Bureau for Educational Visits & Exchanges Seymour Mews House, Seymour Mews, London W1H 9PE ☏ 071-486 5101 offer Project Europe travel bursaries of up to N£200 to those aged 16-19, in full or part-time (but not higher) education to assist in carrying out a study project in another EC country. The bursaries aim to help young people gain international experience when they are preparing to enter the world of work or continue their studies, and to discover some aspects of life in another country related to the applicant's course of study or future employment. Joint projects (up to 3 people) considered.

Christians Abroad 1 Stockwell Green, London SW9 9HP ☏ 071-737 7811 is an ecumenical body funded by aid and mission agencies, providing an information and advisory service on work abroad to help volunteers discover opportunities related to their skills, age, aims and circumstances. Publish a variety of information leaflets giving details of opportunities in Britain and overseas.

Council for International Educational Exchange 33 Seymour Place, London W1H 6AT ☏ 071-706 3008 is a private, non-profitmaking organisation founded in the United States in 1947 to promote international education. Administers a wide range of study, work and travel programmes including opportunities for summer session study at universities in the US, and semester or academic year programmes at various universities worldwide.

Expedition Advisory Centre of the Royal Geographical Society 1 Kensington Gore, London SW7 2AR ☏ 071-581 2057 was jointly founded by the Royal Geographical Society and the Young Explorers' Trust, and is funded by Shell International Petroleum Company under a six-year agreement. Offers information and training for those planning an expedition overseas, running training seminars and providing a service to scientific and youth expeditions, adventure projects, those wishing to join an expedition, and independent and overland travellers.

Gabbitas, Truman & Thring Educational Trust 6, 7 & 8 Sackville Street, London W1X 2BR ☏ 071-734 0161 is a non-profitmaking company offering expert advice and guidance to parents and students covering the choice of independent schools, colleges and courses; planning and preparing for higher education; career guidance and options for a year out.

Local education authorities will be able to provide information on grants available for various types of courses. Listed in the local phone directory under the name of the county, borough or metropolitan council.

National Association of Volunteer Bureaux St Peter's College, College Road, Saltley, Birmingham B8 3TE ✆ 021-327 0265 was set up to serve and represent Britain's volunteer bureaux and to promote volunteering in general. Does not recruit volunteers but can put enquirers in touch with their local volunteer bureau, who will be able to advise them of the entire range of voluntary work available locally.

National Youth Agency 17-23 Albion Street, Leicester LE1 6GD ✆ Leicester (0533) 471200 houses a comprehensive collection of resources on work with young people and the issues that affect them. Can provide information on community involvement and young volunteer organisations in England and Wales.

Odyssey International 21 Cambridge Road, Waterbeach, Cambridge CB4 9NJ ✆ Cambridge (0223) 861079 is a travel club which aims to match like-minded travelling partners. An advice line is run by members who have just returned from abroad giving details of visa problems, vaccination requirements and employment prospects. Publishes a quarterly newsletter detailing travel offers. Annual membership £20.

The Princes Trust 8 Bedford Row, London WC1R 4BA ✆ 071-430 0524 offers approximately 150 *Go and See* grants per year, open to individuals under 26, no longer in full-time education, with ideas for European partnerships in arts and crafts, design, the environment, media and new technology. The grant, maximum £500, can be used to visit potential partners in Europe, discuss and put together a proposal for a joint venture and possibly apply for a *Go Ahead* grant later to actually finance the project. Through its local

committees the Trust also runs 10 month-long Community Ventures aimed at offering young people the chance to become better citizens through the medium of voluntary community service.

Returned Volunteer Action 1 Amwell Street, London EC1R 1UL ✆ 071-278 0804 provides information and advice for those thinking about volunteering overseas, and helps returned volunteers to make use of their overseas experience in Britain by providing support and advice, training courses in communications skills and a channel through which volunteers can comment on and influence the policies of the sending agencies.

Scottish Community Education Council (SCEC) West Coates House, 90 Haymarket Terrace, Edinburgh EH12 5LQ ✆ 031-313 2488 promotes community involvement and service by young people in Scotland. Although it does not recruit volunteers or find places for them, it provides an information sheet giving details of volunteer projects in Scotland, including conservation work, workcamps, community projects, playschemes and some opportunities for long-term volunteers.

USEFUL PUBLICATIONS

Taking a year between
Opportunities in the Gap Year £3 looks at what is available to sixth-formers wishing to take a break between school and university or college. It weighs up the pros and cons of a year between and gives hints on how to make the best of a once-in-a-lifetime opportunity. Published by the Independent Schools Careers Organisation, 12a-18a Princess Way, Camberley, Surrey GU15 3SP ✆ Camberley (0276) 21188.

A Year Off...A Year On? £4.25 is a guide to temporary jobs, voluntary service, vacation jobs, study courses, scholarships, travel and expeditions, available from Careers Research and Advisory Centre (CRAC) Publications,

Hobsons plc, Bateman Street, Cambridge CB2 1LZ © Cambridge (0223) 464334.

Taking A Year Off £7.95 takes a new look at the option of taking a year off before, during or after higher education or during employment, encouraging the reader to identify his or her own needs by placing emphasis on case studies, group discussions and interviews, letters, a quiz, checklists, and the experiences of young people who have taken time out. Published by Trotman and Company Limited, 12-14 Hill Rise, Richmond, Surrey TW10 6UA.

Paid and voluntary work
Working Holidays £7.95 is an annual guide to over 99,000 paid and voluntary seasonal work opportunities in 70 countries. Full information is given on the jobs available together with details on work/residence permits, travel, insurance, accommodation and further sources of information. Published by the Central Bureau for Educational Visits & Exchanges, see below.

Volunteer Work £3.00 is a comprehensive guide to medium and long-term voluntary service with details on over 100 organisations recruiting volunteers for projects in Britain and 153 countries worldwide. Published by the Central Bureau for Educational Visits & Exchanges, Seymour Mews House, Seymour Mews, London W1H 9PE © 071-486 5101. Central Bureau publications are available from all good bookshops or direct by mail; add £1 postage and packing for each title.

International Directory of Volunteer Work £6.95 is a guide to short and long-term volunteer opportunities in Britain and abroad. Published by Vacation Work, 9 Park End Street, Oxford OX1 1HJ © Oxford (0865) 241978.

Directory of Work & Study in Developing Countries £7.95 is a guide to employment, voluntary work and academic opportunities in the Third World for those who wish to experience life there not just as a tourist. Published by Vacation Work, *see above.*

Directory of Summer Jobs Abroad £6.95 including UK postage, is an annual publication detailing vacancies in over 40 countries, including information on jobs offered, wages given and addresses of employees. Published by Vacation Work, *see above.*

Directory of Summer Jobs in Britain £6.95 lists opportunities all over Britain with details of wages and hours, conditions of work and qualifications required. Published by Vacation Work, *see above.*

Summer Employment Directory of the United States £8.95 gives details of thousands of summer jobs for students in the US and Canada. Includes a section giving advice on legal requirements and visa procedure for non-US citizens. Published by Writer's Digest Books and available in the UK through Vacation Work, *see above.*

Internships USA, £15.95 lists career-oriented positions enabling students and graduates to train through a period of work with an established employer. Published by Writer's Digest Books and available in the UK through Vacation Work, *see above.*

Emplois d'Été en France lists thousands of vacancies for summer jobs in France. Also includes special information for foreign students, with details of authorisation on working in France. Published by Vac-job, Paris, and available in the UK through Vacation Work, *see above,* price £6.95.

Sponsorships
Vac Work £1 gives details of vacation work, sandwich placements, training and other types of employment available to undergraduates during the vacations. The main issues are published in February and November and supplements are available during the academic year. Published by

Central Services Unit for Graduate Careers Services. Available for consultation in university, polytechnic or college careers information rooms, or direct from CSU, Armstrong House, Oxford Road, Manchester M1 7EQ.

Sponsorships 92 £3.31 including postage, lists sponsorships offered to students by employers and professional bodies for first degrees, BTEC and SCOTVEC higher awards or comparable courses. Available from the Careers and Occupational Information Centre, Rockery Cottage, Sutton-cum-Lound, Retford, Nottinghamshire DN22 8PJ ✆ Retford (0777) 705951.

Sponsorship and Training Opportunities in Engineering, free, details sponsorships and training offered to 6th form or college students applying for university or polytechnic engineering degree courses and for final year engineering degree students seeking a graduate training post. Published annually in July and available from the Institute of Mechanical Engineers, PO Box 23, Northgate Avenue, Bury St Edmunds IP32 6BN ✆ Bury St Edmunds (0284) 763277.

Students and Sponsorship £4.95, is an annual publication dealing with aspects of course sponsorship by employers. It looks at the range of options available to students about to enter further and higher education at a time when employers are concerned to recruit the best employees from a shrinking pool. Available from Careers Research and Advisory Centre (CRAC) Publications, Hobsons plc, Bateman Street, Cambridge CB2 1LZ ✆ Cambridge (0223) 464334.

Further study and grants

Home From Home £6.99 is an authoritative guide to over 120 organisations arranging homestays, exchanges, home exchanges, farm stays and term stays in more than 50 countries. At a time when travellers are turning away from the alienation of mass

tourism, the guide offers a wide selection of responsible alternatives. Published by the Central Bureau for Educational Visits & Exchanges, see below.

Study Holidays £7.95, (1992 edition) contains full information on courses in over 20 European languages, from one week to one academic year. The guide also contains practical information on accommodation, travel, sources for bursaries, grants and scholarships and useful publications. Published by the Central Bureau for Educational Visits & Exchanges and available from all good bookshops or direct from the Bureau (add £1 each title for post and packing).

Directory of Independent Further Education £3.60, contains basic information on over 2,500 colleges and training establishments. Colleges are grouped in nine sections, from those offering tutorial courses through to those offering more specialist courses. Published by the Independent Schools Careers Organisation, *see above*, and available from Careers Research and Advisory Centre (CRAC) Publications, Hobsons plc, Bateman Street, Cambridge CB2 1LZ ✆ Cambridge (0223) 464334.

Higher Education in the European Community: The Student Handbook £13.95 contains information on the facilities and courses offered by the twelve EC member states. It looks at higher education systems throughout the Community and provides invaluable information for those wishing to study in an EC member country. Published by the Office of Official Publications of the European Communities, and available in the UK from Trotman and Company Limited, 12 Hill Rise, Richmond, Surrey TW10 6UA ✆ 081-332 2132.

Study Abroad XXVI 1989-91 £12.50 lists over 200,000 scholarships, fellowships, assistantships and travel grants at university level throughout the world. Published by UNESCO, 7 Place de Fontenoy, 75700 Paris,

France, and obtainable in the UK from HMSO ✆ 071-873 0011.

Scholarships Abroad, published annually, lists over 270 scholarships tenable for a full academic year to British students by overseas governments and universities as well as a number of bursaries for shorter periods. The majority of awards are for postgraduates only. Published by the British Council, 65 Davies Street, London W1Y 2AA ✆ 071-930 8466.

Charities Digest £10.95 is a useful publication listing a number of educational charities. Published by the Family Welfare Association, 501/505 Kingsland Road, London E8 4AU ✆ 071-254 6251.

Directory of Grant-Making Trusts £49.50 is a list of voluntary grant-making bodies in England and Wales covering all fields of voluntary activities including medicine and health, welfare, education, the sciences and humanities, religion and the environment. Published by Charities Aid Foundation, 48 Pambury Road, Tonbridge, Kent TN9 2JD ✆ Tonbridge (0732) 771333.

Grants To Students, free, explains higher education grants available from LEAs. It details what the grant covers, who is eligible, how to apply, and is available from LEAs or from the Department of Education & Science, Sanctuary Buildings, Great Smith Street, London SW1P 3BT ✆ 071-925 5000.

The Grants Register 1991-1993 covers scholarships, fellowships and research grants; exchange opportunities, vacation study awards and travel grants; grants for artistic or scientific projects; competitions, prizes, honoraria; professional and vocational awards, and awards for refugees, minority groups and students in unexpected financial difficulties. Published by Macmillan, Stockton House, Melbourne House, Aldwych, London WC2B 4LF ✆ 071-836 6633.

Expeditions and general travel
Expedition Planners' Handbook and Directory 1991-92 £12.95 is the best and most comprehensive guide to all aspects of expedition planning with articles by over forty specialists from the world of science and exploration. Includes sections on research, adventure, charity, community and youth projects; planning, logistics and techniques; plus directories of reference sources, grant-giving bodes and equipment suppliers. Several of the chapters are available for sale as individual booklets, including *Fund-Raising for Expeditions* £2.50, *Insurance for Expeditions* £1.50, *Reference Sources for Expeditions* £2.50, and *Guide to Writing Reports* £1.50. Published by the Expedition Advisory Centre, *see above.*

Fundraising to Join an Expedition £1.50 is a guide for those raising the funds required to join ventures such as Operation Raleigh. Published by the Expedition Advisory Centre, *see above.*

Joining an Expedition £4 details how to take advantage of the expedition opportunities offered by over fifty UK-based organisations, with fundraising advice. Published by the Expedition Advisory Centre, *see above.*

Sources of Information for Independent and Overland Travellers £3 is a reference guide giving details on where to get the best information about health, equipment, visas, insurance, maps, and so on. Published by the Expedition Advisory Centre, *see above.*

The Travellers' Handbook is a reference and source book for the independent traveller, with chapters on travel, camping and backpacking, hitch-hiking, health, clothing, where to stay, dealing with people when things go wrong, photography, choosing maps, passports, visas, permits, insurance, currency and Customs. Also includes special chapters for students, single women and people with a disability. Published by WEXAS International 45-49 Brompton Road,

London SW3 1DE ℂ 071-589 0500, price £11.95 (£6.95 to members).

Lonely Planet's *Travel Survival Kits* are detailed handbooks to countries in Africa, Asia, Australasia and the Americas, giving background on the country, advice on places to visit information on where to stay, what to eat, how to get there and ways to travel around. Available in most good bookshops and distributed in the UK by Roger Lascelles, 47 York Road, Brentford, Middlesex TW8 0QP. Prices range from £4.95-£13.95.

Rough Guides are a series of practical handbooks to most countries in Europe and some areas of Asia, Africa, South America and the United States, giving full details on cities, towns and places of interest, plus a wealth of practical information on places to stay and how to get around. The range also includes *Women Travel*, a guide for women travellers; also *Nothing Ventured: disabled people travel the world* containing first-hand accounts of disabled people's travel experiences and practical advice on planning a trip. Published by Harrap Columbus, Chelsea House, 26 Market Square, Bromley, Kent BR1 1NA and available in most good bookshops. Prices range from £4.95-£9.95.

Culture Shock! is a series of cultural guides written for international travellers of any background. The reader is introduced to the people, customs, ceremonies, food and culture of a country, with checklists of dos and don'ts. Countries currently in the series include Australia, Canada, China, France, Indonesia, Israel, Japan, Malaysia, Pakistan, the Philippines, Singapore, Thailand and the USA; further countries forthcoming. All guides cost £6.95 and are available from good bookshops or through Kuperard (London) Ltd, 30 Cliff Road, London NW1 9AG ℂ 071-284 0512.

A Year Between is published by the Central Bureau for Educational Visits & Exchanges, the UK national office responsible for the provision of information and advice on all forms of educational visits and exchanges; the development and administration of a wide range of curriculum-related pre-service and in-service exchange programmes; the linking of educational establishments and local education authorities with counterparts abroad; and the organisation of meetings, workshops and conferences related to professional international experience. Its information and advisory services extend throughout the educational field. In addition, over 25,000 indivdual enquiries are answered each year. Publications cater for the needs of people of all ages seeking information on the various opportunities available for educational contacts and travel abroad.

The Central Bureau was established in 1948 by the British government and is funded by the Department of Education & Science, the Scottish Office Education Department and the Department of Education for Northern Ireland.

Chairman of the Board: JA Carter
Director: AH Male
Deputy Director: WE Musk

Seymour Mews House
Seymour Mews
London W1H 9PE
ℂ 071-486 5101
Telex 21368 CBEVEX
Fax 071-935 5741

3 Bruntsfield Crescent
Edinburgh EH10 4HD
ℂ 031-447 8024
Fax 031-452 8569

16 Malone Road
Belfast BT9 5BN
ℂ 0232-664418/9
Fax 0232-661275

Polly Gillingham, on a year between through GAP Activity Projects, teaches a class of children in a remote village in Nepal

Throughout this guide, in the sections on practical information and advice and in the individual sections on placements there are accounts from students and employing and placing organisations alike. As wide-ranging as the experiences are, the underlying message is that for those concerned a year between gave a positive impetus to their personal development, future studies and eventual careers.

In this section we asked five quite different organisations, GAP Activity Projects, The Missions to Seamen, Operation Raleigh, Project Trust and The Year In Industry to recount the values they place in a year between and to highlight just some of the experiences of students they place.

From the immense appreciation of a village community in Pakistan to the invaluable recognition of a British engineering company, from the warmth of working with seafarers in Japan to the frozen challenge of an expedition in Alaska, from Christmas dinner of pheasant in Egypt to a close encounter with a shark attack victim in the South China Sea, these reports are vital testaments for all those considering taking a year between.

THE BENEFITS OF A YEAR BETWEEN

John Spencer, Assistant Director of GAP Activity Projects explains how a mixed bag of work and travel can lead to self-discovery and greater maturity. GAP is an educational charity, founded in 1972 to give those with a year between leaving school and going on to higher education or vocational training the opportunity to travel to another country and live and work among its people.

The concept of a year between school and higher education has gained rapidly in momentum during recent years with the result that there is now a growing trend among young people to step aside from formal education for a year or more before proceeding to university courses or professional education. This swing is likely to become even more marked during the 1990s as more school leavers are expected to exercise their initiative and enterprise in hunting out work and travel opportunities, both in the UK and overseas. By so doing they show their resolve to increase their awareness of people and places and to acquire a new dimension of maturity and independence.

A recent survey has indicated that already at least 25% of those currently entering higher education prefer to have a break of varying duration between school and college. Those who have grown weary of A level pressures and the attendant problems of university entrance may see a year between as a chance to recharge the batteries before the final challenge of a degree/diploma course. At a time of economic recession some may find it necessary to raise funds to help them through their student years. Others may have a burning ambition to broaden their vision by undertaking challenging work in some distant part of the world where lifestyles are different and a culture shock can be a stimulus to a new thinking. Whatever individual motives may be, the year between, if carefully planned and constructively used, can be an excellent foundation for gaining a more balanced approach to higher education and thereby reaping greater benefit from it.

At one time universities and colleges were a shade cautious about welcoming the newly emerging phenomenon of a year between with open arms. There was still an old guard who favoured an unbroken progression from school to college and the argument was often put forward that those who opted for an intervening year were in danger of losing touch with the process of learning and might even forget much of what they had learned at school. However in the world of higher education there is now little support among lecturers and teachers for this view. In a few areas of study - mathematics and music are sometimes quoted - the importance of continuity is still sometimes mentioned but the prevailing opinion now is that the advantages of a constructive year between considerably outweigh the disadvantages.

A wide variety of work is available to those who decide on a year between. In many countries there is an increasing desire to learn the English language and volunteers on a year between frequently help to meet this demand, especially if they have been able to undertake a short TEFL course. There are a considerable number of placements round the world for young people who are willing to throw themselves enthusiastically into the general life of a residential school community. Such volunteers need to come to terms with the fact that they are no longer pupils but junior members of staff: this adjustment can often generate a greater awareness of responsibility and lead to a positive involvement with the sporting and cultural activities of a school. Domestic duties (assisting with meals, supervising dormitories and helping with the maintenance of playing-fields) are often thrown in for good measure and most volunteers learn, if they have not already done so, to take the rough with the smooth. Apart from school placements there are also openings at home and abroad for social and community work, for work experience in the business world, on farms, in hotels, in conservation work and in adventure training establishments.

In all these situations it is usual for board and accommodation to be offered - and sometimes a limited amount of pocket money - but the financial costs of the year between need to be carefully considered. There are no grants from public funds and volunteers must therefore be prepared to pay for all their travelling expenses, insurance and any fees. The final figure depends largely on the distance travelled: schemes in Australia, New Zealand, India, Africa, the Americas and the Far East are likely to incur expenditure of £1,500-£2,000 . Projects in European countries - and there are now increasing opportunities in eastern Europe - will probably involve a slightly smaller outlay. Despite the current recession it is very heartening to see the initiative shown in raising the necessary funds. Although parents do sometimes make a contribution, the majority of year between students prefer to be independent and to collect the necessary resources by their own individual efforts through holiday employment and sponsorship. There have been many instances of school leavers from restricted home backgrounds who have shown remarkable tenacity in overcoming this financial problem. For them the fruits of the year between will be even greater; they will have demonstrated at an early age a degree of commitment which is likely to play a big part in shaping their character in later years.

When the final balance sheet is drawn up, what are the main benefits of the year between and who are the beneficiaries? It would seem that those who benefit fall into three groups. Universities and polytechnics gain from the added input of students who have been out in the real world and have educated themselves in the school of life. They will have greater motivation for their studies and will be less likely to pull out during or after the first year. For it is not uncommon for universities and colleges to have problems with younger and less mature students, who go direct from school into higher education and then have doubts and misgivings about their choice of course. Some research has been done on the eventual attainments of those who have taken a year away from formal training. The conclusion has been that such people do better both in academic results and in the likelihood of completing the course than the mass of their contemporaries.

Employers too can fairly claim to be beneficiaries of the year between. They are frequently to be heard stressing the importance of work experience and several captains of industry have publicly stressed the relevance of a constructive in-between year. The ability to relate to other people and to show initiative in dealing with practical problems is much valued by prospective employers. In this country the curriculum for potential graduates is often both shorter and narrower than elsewhere and this makes it even more desirable for young people to seize every opportunity of gaining wider experience in the outside world. A former chairman of BP has confirmed this:

BP is consistent in promulgating its message that academic achievement by itself is not the key to success and therefore can only welcome initiatives which broaden the outlook of young people and equip them better for their adult life.

But, of course, the greatest beneficiaries are those young people who decide to defer college entry for a year and to embark on a work/travel programme for their own enrichment. A few of their own comments will serve by way of illustration. A young man from Scotland spent his year between working on a farm in Australia and then touring the country:

The main benefit of this year was to prepare me for university which I knew I wasn't ready for when I left school.

Another volunteer was placed in Israel to work on a kibbutz near Nazareth. She worked in the bakery, often late at night:

When I decided to go to the kibbutz I considered that it would be a means of seeing the Holy Land but the kibbutz itself turned out to be the main focus of my time

in Israel. I have no regrets at having taken time off between school and university to do something entirely different.

Another year between volunteer was assigned to Barclays Bank in Rouen, where she found that her duties as a cashier were too varied to fall into a predictable pattern:

It required a sense of organisation, an ability to do many things simultaneously and a fair degree of patience. I would find it hard to thank Barclays and GAP enough for the chance of a lifetime which they gave me.

Two volunteers who left school in June 1991 are currently at a Cheshire Home in Malaysia caring for the handicapped residents:

We are still enjoying every minute of it. The residents here are such fantastic people. They are all so individual and have great personalities. We love working with them as they have so much to offer.

A penetrating and thoughtful report came from a volunteer who worked in a preparatory school. She summarised the effect of a year between as follows:

I not only gained in experience but grew mentally, becoming more independent and learning more about myself. Being away from family and friends broadens your mind - you find out who you are and what you would like to become. I now feel more independent and have the confidence to make decisions for myself and by myself.

These comments from young people who have taken a year between could be multiplied many times over. Experience shows that the large majority have put the time to excellent use and have been able to develop a social awareness which has enabled them to be of service, to become more self-reliant and to have a clearer picture of their objectives in life. For them it will have been a most memorable and formative year.

A YEAR OF CHALLENGE

Jan Burbery, from The Missions to Seamen, describes how a placement as a Mission chaplain's assistant in the year between offers the challenge of practical Christian service. The Missions to Seamen is an Anglican missionary founded in 1856, caring for the spiritual and material welfare of seafarers around the globe. The Missions help to combat isolation, exploitation and the dangers of the sea, working for improvements in conditions, education and welfare, offering a ministry of word, sacrament, counselling care and Christian welcome.

It was exciting and interesting. I got the chance to meet people from all over the world; people from cultures I didn't know anything about. At the same time it was hard work, it was tiring, it could be frustrating and sometimes it was sad seeing the conditions in which seafarers work and the lives they live.

But all in all I wouldn't have missed it for anything; it's an experience I will treasure for the rest of my life.

This was how Jacob Knee described his year working in a seafarers' club as a student assistant with The Missions to Seamen. He went to Dunkerque after being accepted for the society's voluntary service scheme which offers 18-24 year olds the opportunity to become involved in practical Christian service within the shipping industry.

The scheme provides chaplains at the Mission's Flying Angel clubs in 20 of the busier ports with much needed help, and gives student assistants the chance to learn about and help others in an environment with a truly international flavour.

They help chaplains in most aspects of their work and they have to be prepared to do anything from visiting seafarers on board ship, welcoming them at the club, helping them make phone calls home, changing money, running the shop and, not least, providing a sympathetic ear and helping with a problem.

Student assistants also have to be prepared to go anywhere. It could be to the heat and dust of the far flung Australian mining community in Dampier or the tropical lushness of Mombasa. It could be across the Channel to Rotterdam or Dunkerque, or across the Atlantic to New Orleans.

On the other hand, it might be to comparatively familiar surroundings in a UK port. Former volunteer Jonathan Allat:

I had hoped to spend a year abroad, so I was disappointed when I was posted to Southampton, but the multi-national, multi-cultural clientele at the Mission meant the world came to me. I spoke to British seafarers in transit to and from the Gulf war, Indians at the time of Gandhi's assassination, and Yugoslavians when their civil war started.

Meeting and talking with seafarers is a large part of the work, and this often takes place during a visit aboard ship - a job which can be daunting when first undertaken.

Kirsty Fraser wrote from Kobe:

Visiting ships proved quite a challenge and at first I found it a little nerve wracking having no idea who I would meet at the top of the gangway! But as it became much more familiar, I felt that my approach improved with my self-confidence.

You diced with death walking up dodgy gangplanks, wrote another volunteer, *prayed that the ship wouldn't sail while you were on board, struggled to explain in pidgin English where the club was. The reception would vary from disinterest to being the centre of attention in an excited crowd clamouring for leaflets.*

Working with people from so many different countries and cultures is one of the experiences volunteers find most valuable. The comments made by this student after his year with the Mission are echoed by many:

On a personal level I feel I have grown up considerably. I have seen, and have some understanding of, situations that I never knew existed. I feel more aware of myself, my weaknesses and my strong points, and I am more able to converse with anyone.

Certainly, as a student assistant with the Mission you have to be prepared to cope with a large variety of new experiences. You may be far from home, living in a different culture and you will have to come to terms with the fast-moving modern shipping industry and its international personnel.

But these experiences help student assistants understand the problems and experiences of the seafarers themselves. When they are at sea, seafarers are completely isolated from the community ashore. When in port - for periods of time made ever briefer by more efficient cargo handling techniques - they often find themselves in places where they feel alienated by language and culture.

When Sophie Gregory was sent to Brisbane she had times when she missed her home and family and as a result she really appreciated how seafarers would miss theirs:

The difference was that for me it was only a year, for them it's a way of life. And at least my family was at the end of a phone.

On a more practical level Aiden Kennedy wrote from Fremantle:

I had to learn to run up and down Japanese tuna boats without knocking my head off, drive into town to find lost seafarers and do airport runs in the middle of the night, as well as learn the ropes as club duty officer which meant handling foreign money, bookkeeping, cooking meals for seafarers and so on. But if I thought I was thrown in the deep end when I started this job, imagine how seafarers feel arriving in Fremantle speaking no English, with no clue where they are - strangers in a strange country. They are in at the deep end, not me.

An important part of the job is being open to seafarers needs. You may get very specific requests, such as being asked to arrange a football match for a crew or to help in a justice case such as non-payment of wages.

But more often it is a question of offering friendship and spending time talking and listening. It may not seem very much, but to seafarers far from home, it can mean a great deal that someone cares enough to spend time with them. One student wrote:

By simply giving an hour of my time and listening to them, no matter how mundane the conversation, seemed to be a way of expressing that they had value. I came to appreciate the importance of listening ... I began to see the need to listen to someone telling their story, not in order to better it or to contradict it, but to hear what they were trying to express. The challenge of becoming a better listener remained with me throughout. I became aware of the reciprocal nature of many exchanges with seafarers. Far from me giving something, it was more a question of vice-versa, for often, in the warm welcome of a group of badly treated men, I experienced glimpses of God's joy.

For others, self development came with taking on more responsibility than had dreamed of before they left home. In one club, the two assistants were to run the club in the chaplain's two week absence ... and then one broke his leg.

It suddenly dawned on me that I would be running the club alone, said the other later. A mixture of fear and excitement followed. The first week was the busiest since I had started work and I didn't get home before 11 pm any evening . But the second was a complete contrast and the enemy was loneliness. During that time I learned a lot about myself. Unsure at first, I found myself capable of more than I expected.

Almost without exception, returning student assistants talk of the benefits of learning a lot about themselves, usually as a result of the demands of the job, and gaining self-confidence as a result. Many of them feel that they gained as much, if not more, than the people they have been sent out to help.

The most important feature of the Missions' work is the visit of the chaplain and staff to each ship on its arrival in port. Above right, Kirsty Fraser, a student assistant with the Missions on her year between, ship visiting in Kobe, Japan. Right, Simon Swallow was also a student assistant in his year between. Here he talks with a seafarer in Hong Kong harbour.

THE EXPEDITION EXPERIENCE

Richard Snailham from Operation Raleigh profiles the opportunities that an expedition experience can offer, to the volunteers themselves, from whatever background, and to the communities they help along the route. Operation Raleigh aims to provide a unique opportunity for young people of many nations to develop their self-confidence and leadership skills by stretching themselves mentally and physically in the service of others.

There is so much debate whether it is better to take a year between school and university or after university, or even if it is a good idea to have one at all. Amanda Salmon, a chirpy 22 year-old from Glastonbury, reckons that taking a year out helped her to grow out of the uniformity of school life to her present confidence and individuality. She left Millfield in June 1987 with three modest A levels and no place yet at any university. So she applied for and managed to pass the exacting Operation Raleigh selection test. Her second challenge was to raise the required £2,000 in the six months before her expedition to Pakistan. She took part in that summer's annual Operation Raleigh Round Britain Bike Ride and earned £300 pedalling from Lincoln to London. She confesses that she chose that stage because it was flatter! A stint on a sales counter at Harrods raised some more.

Eventually in April 1988, she left, with forty others from Britain, the United States, Canada, Singapore and of course Pakistan, on the three month long venture. As with every Raleigh expedition the time was spent on three sorts of activity - community project work, scientific research and adventure.

Amanda first set to work building a house at an orphanage in Dhodial in the North West Frontier province. The stones were horribly rough but with the help of two Pakistanis, who spoke only Urdu, the house was completed before June.

A medical project came next. Donning a white coat and after a short course to familiarise her with a stethoscope, Amanda began screening the hundreds of villagers who presented themselves with suspected tuberculosis.

Even though this was quite a small expedition by Operation Raleigh standards there were several scientific projects available. The

Islamabad Natural History Museum asked for a collection of flora and amphibians to be made for them. Amanda went on the hunt for toads, newts, scorpions and the like but her softness of heart occasionally overcame her zeal for science and rather than subject them to death by formaldehyde, she sometimes let them go.

At Changla Gali she took part in a Rhesus monkey survey and for the Royal Society for the Protection of Birds a survey was attempted of the Western Tragopan pheasant, but unhappily none was seen. Most Operation Raleigh expeditions are adventurous by the very nature of the terrain they take place in and the fact that the venturers generally have to trek from one project to another. But there are often special excitements built in and for Amanda it was a three-week trek to the base camp of the 8,126 metre Nanga Parbat.

Before going to Pakistan, during the money-raising stage, she had secured a place to read geography at University College, London. Ask her what she thinks the Raleigh experience did for her and she positively bubbles with enthusiasm:

It may sound a cliché, but it made me a more rounded, forward-thinking person, and I know I'm biased, but I think being picked for Raleigh helped me to get into UCL; it was a definite plus point at the interview.

One of her fellow venturers in Pakistan was a cheerful, chain-smoking little Mersysider called Sara Beesley. Amanda, raised in rural Somerset, had rarely seen someone like Sara with her spikes of dyed blonde hair, outrageous earrings and way-out dress. Yet they became firm mates:

From my somewhat sheltered background it was good to meet some of the Youth Development Programme people. About 20% of every expedition now are disadvantaged in some way.

After Pakistan Amanda back-packed around China for three months, returning in late September in time to get ready for UCL:

Fending for myself in China made me more self reliant still. And when I got to university I noticed the difference between those who'd had a year between and those who hadn't. The year out people seemed to have a more highly developed moral sense. The non-year betweeners spent the first months in an alcoholic haze while I feel the year between types were more responsible about this and used their freedom sensibly and knew what lectures to go to.

She emerged with a 2:1.

The Operation Raleigh expedition experience offers threefold benefits: to the venturers, to the scientists whom the venturers help, and to the overseas community they work in.

The qualities which Operation Raleigh seeks to give - a sense of responsibility to self and to others, resolve, and the ability to lead - bring out the very best in the young people who participate.

It seems that the challenges of being selected, gathering funds and surviving an expedition constitute an excellent way of spending the year between.

A final testimonial comes from some Pakistani villagers for whom Operation Raleigh worked on a road project:

Words are insufficient to express our heartfelt thanks for your contribution ... in constructing a link road over the steep ground. It was a challenging task and needed tremendous muscular effort. We know that you were never used to such kind of manual labour in such a terrain. The most astonishing factor in this enterprise has been the indomitable will of the females who worked side by side with the males of the group and never lagged behind them.

© ORPIX

Amanda Salmon working alongside the locals, building a house at the SOS orphanage in Dhodial, North West Frontier province, Pakistan

Notwithstanding all these facts, with complete disregard of personal comforts, you collectively plunged into the valley of dust and like a driving shaft of a locomotive went forward by removing heavy boulders, shovelling aside tons of earth, brought down many trees, hammered down heavy rocks and at last, in a record time of just fifteen days, turned a boulder-infested barren land strip into a first class wagonable road.

Your team, we know, was never after any money from our underdeveloped town. Purely on humanitarian grounds you have helped us with the sacred intention of raising our living standard. This road which you have constructed for us, in days ahead, will lighten our burden of pulling up rations and other loads from miles down. Kindly convey our very warm thanks and our very best regards to the heads of your respective states and your illustrious parents who, so precisely, educated you to serve mankind in any part of the world.

During the course of your tasks here, if anyone of us has erroneously uttered any unpleasant word, please pardon us. Wherever you go, we pray for you to be happy all your life. Goodbye, go ahead and God speed you.

A YEAR OF ADVENTURE

The Project Trust aims to enable a new generation to experience life and work overseas, gaining some understanding of life outside Europe, particularly in the Third World, and places British school leavers on a year between as volunteers in a way which is of real benefit to the community. Here Lavinia Bristol, Project's Administrator follows two applicants on their year of adventure.

Michael Guest from Newcastle and Ben Bridge from Buckinghamshire are both living and working on the Isle of Coll in the Inner Hebrides at present as group leaders for the organisation which they joined a year ago, which offered them a challenging and exciting year of adventure.

Both applied to Project Trust in the autumn of 1989. Michael applied because he knew he did not want to go into higher education straight away and he wanted to explore the wide world beyond the north of England. Ben was determined to join the Navy, but wanted to spend a year beforehand analysing his own motives for doing this. He wanted as varied a year as possible and saw Project as the way to do it.

Ben says that his parents were impressed with the back up and support offered by Project Trust. His mother, in particular, was concerned that he was going so far away but she was keen that he should spend a full year abroad.

A stiff selection course on the Isle of Coll in the spring of 1990 strengthened the boys' resolve, and gave them a confidence in their own ability to face the year ahead. Ben says:

It was reassuring to know that an organisation with Project's experience felt I was capable of doing a job overseas. They offered me a place at the Outward Bound School in Hong Kong, and I was thrilled - it was just what I wanted.

Michael accepted a place teaching English to adults at a language school in Egypt:

I was pleased by my acceptance but apprehensive about the remoteness of the project. I knew nothing about Egypt, even less about teaching the English language.

Michael and Ben returned to Coll in July 1990 for a week's training course. Michael learnt to teach and Ben was given a grounding in various Outward Bound activities including canoeing, climbing and instruction in teaching techniques. In addition they learnt about their different projects, the country, how to look after themselves, what to do if they fell ill, and even how to look below the surface of their projects to get the most out of their year.

Ben travelled out by sea, thanks to Ben Line who offered him a place on a container ship sailing through Suez to Hong Kong. Michael travelled more mundanely by air. Michael says:

I arrived at four in the morning. I was exhausted, and Cairo was like nowhere I have ever seen before. I was overwhelmed by the sounds, and sights, and smells around me - even Newcastle after a football match could not compare with this!

Michael was met by the cousin of his future employer and travelled by train down to Sohag, in Upper Egypt:

My partner, Rupert, and I started teaching the day we arrived. Most of our pupils were university students, young, friendly and really eager to learn. Groups were small and the standard of English was higher than I had imagined. The school itself was pretty disorganised and much of our time was spent drinking glasses of sweet black tea with other members of staff.

It was a curious transition from having been so recently a pupil, to discovering students took me seriously as a member of staff. All the other members of staff tried their best to make us feel at home, although it was not always easy understanding their culture and their language. The first time I thought of Sohag as my home was when I returned to Cairo for a long weekend and the relief of getting back to my friends and the village atmosphere of Sohag was immense.

Ben was one of three from Project Trust to go to the Outward Bound School:

My work was divided into three very distinct parts. The largest sailing vessel in the South China sea was my home for the first two months. The Ji Fung sailed out to the Philippines, and my job as bosun's mate was to help maintain everything on ship, from oiling blocks to stowing sails fifty feet above a heaving deck.

At other times I was on the water front, looking after the school's fleet of boats and helping to maintain the school premises. The third part of my work was on the land courses, working first as an assistant instructor and eventually taking my own groups.

I had problems with a trapped nerve in my arm in the autumn, and I really appreciated then the back up Project gave me. My representative organised a specialist to see me and Project picked up the bill. I also enjoyed the visit by my desk officer who travelled all the way from the Isle of Coll to Hong Kong to see us before he went on to visit the volunteers in China.

I experienced amazing things during my year. I shall never forget the awful moment when I found a decomposing body in the water. I was sailing along happily when I saw this thing, and I could smell it too. It had lost an arm and its chest was ripped open. I was told later it was the victim of a shark attack. That was the most horrendous moment of my year!

Michael too had memorable moments. He particularly remembers his Christmas dinner, the first he had ever spent away from home:

We had it with the boss of ICI Egypt who kindly invited us for our dinner. Compared to the plain home cooking of Sohag the lavish banquet that he gave us was incredible. I had turkey and pheasant

followed by an enormous gateau. It was the best meal I had all year.

Michael and Ben returned in the summer of 1991. Ben says his only regret is that he cannot do it all over again. Michael sums up:

I benefited from my experiences so much that I decided to apply for a job with Project, so I could help others to do the same.

But what of the benefits to the communities that the Project's volunteers are placed in? The Minister of Health in an African state had this to say:

Thank you for conceiving the idea of Project, and to the young people who came here and showed us that we can help ourselves and need rely on no one. Big development schemes from UNO mostly benefit the donors and bond the recipients to perpetual dependence for funds. We are often very terrified of crossing a river beacuse we believe it is deep and we don't know how to swim, when all that is necesary is to wade across, as the water level reaches no higher than our knees.

A Project Trust volunteer, placed on a community development project in her year between, here leads a music lesson at St Peter's Rock School in Jamaica

A HEAD START

Brian Tripp, National Director of The Year In Industry analyses how a year between offers the chance to acquire valuable experience, the chance to earn some money and the opportunity to find yourself in exciting and challenging situations. Moreover, he believes you will probably get a better degree than you would by going straight from school to university and will certainly be more employable as a graduate.

Martin Walton admits that it came as a bit of a surprise just two weeks into his Year in Industry with Hattersley Heaton Ltd when he was asked to design a bellows sealed industrial stop valve. Martin's actual brief was to:

Prepare a design specification to meet the technical and sales needs;
Understand the requirements of national and international standards;
Provide an initial design;
Verify the design by theoretical calculations and by prototype testing;
Make the test equipment and components;
Produce a final design/development report.

Martin himself takes up the story:

This seemed a bit daunting at first even though I knew I would be working with the guidance of one of the senior engineers. Looking back, I really enjoyed the project. A lot of the work was done on the company's computer-aided design system which was useful because prior to this the nearest I'd really got to computers was playing space invaders! During the year I've had quite a lot of practical experience testing various parts of valves. I've been using machinery such as lathes and millers for the first time whenever prototypes have been needed. This has made me appreciate the work that goes into manufacturing parts, which must be taken into account at the design stage of any project. As a result of my year out I feel I've grown up. I've been given responsibilities and as a result I'm better prepared for university. I've had an insight into industry and so hopefully there will be bit more meaning to the course work I'll be doing at Leeds over the next three years.

Martin's work helped Hattersley Heaton introduce a new product to the market in a much shorter timescale than would otherwise have been possible. Personnel Manager Peter Swarbrick describes The Year In Industry as exceedingly good value for money - it put an extra resource into his company's development section cheaply and effectively and for this reason he decided to take part again this year despite a long hard look at company costs and numbers.

Stories like this can be found right across The Year In Industry:

Two students designed and built a car radiator quality checking fixture which saved Llanelli Radiators £62,000 over a full year; (incidentally, they also won an award in the Young Engineers for Britain competition).

One student, working with a major chemical company, devised a system for internal inspection of used steel drums, showing potential savings of at least £250,000.

Another rewrote some of the process control software for a Texaco refinery and had it up and running without the need for the normal £1.5m per day plant closedown!

M Alwyn, chief engineer, AB Electronics:

The Year in Industry performs a vital service by providing access to a pool of high quality and productive undergraduates in a cost effective way.

The Year In Industry scheme targets students in the year between school and university and gives them paid, challenging work in a company backed by comprehensive off-the-job training. It started as a pilot scheme in Bristol in 1986 as the Pre Formation of Undergraduate Engineers and rapidly developed a national network of twelve regions. In 1991 it joined forces with Index, another leading organisation recruiting and placing pre-university students. The prime objective is to attract young people of the highest calibre into industry.

Dr David Last, University College of Wales:

It would be hard to find a more useful way to spend a pre-entry year.

Potential year between students may register with the region of their choice - most students want to work close to where they live but can choose to work away from home if they wish. The scheme's regional directors try to match students to a company, taking account of the type of work they would like and of course the companies' preference on degree discipline, academic record, location and so forth.

If they get an interview and offer of appointment then the student will be paid the going rate for young people for the company they join (subject to a minimum, for example £110 per week in 1991).

Fiona Foster, student at TI Reynolds Rings and UMIST:

It was the best thing I could have done - the experience of industry, the real world and people. More students should be encouraged.

To help students adjust quickly and contribute effectively to their new working environment, Year in Industry staff organise more than twenty days of seminars and workshops on subjects like communication, design, finance, marketing, project planning and so on. Throughout the year students will have access to personal tutors to advise and assist as required.

Most of the placements are engineering or science based but students of all disciplines are welcome as there are opportunities also to work in companies' marketing, personnel or finance departments, for example.

Companies use the year to assess students as future employees, so many are offered sponsorship at the end of their year. This way both students and companies can get to know each other before making any commitment and of course companies find they can make better use of their limited sponsorship funds.

Some companies take a really imaginative approach. Renold Conveyor for example gave Peter Sherwin a grant and asked him to investigate manufacturing processes on their behalf during his mechanical design and mathematics course at Nottingham University. Peter will be looking for ideas to improve Renold's manufacturing flexibility or reduce lead times. Manufacturing engineering manager Alan Smith says:

This way the company gets a direct benefit from Peter's sponsorship as well as forging links with the university's faculties; and of course Peter sees that he is useful to the company.

Looking back on their experience, Year In Industry students usually say that it boosted their personal development and helped them make more informed decisions about higher education and careers. As graduates, they achieve spectacular results: so far, 24% have got firsts and 40% upper seconds - well above the national norm - and that goes for all students, even those whose A level results were officially classified as below average.

75% of Year In Industry students were employed by industry immediately after graduation. A further 14% have taken higher degrees and expect to return to industry later. On the evidence to date the scheme appears to produce more mature, more committed undergraduates, better equipped to achieve on their degree course and in their career.

Steven Osborn, student at Inmos and Oxford:

My year was very worthwhile indeed. I wish more A level students could see the light and take a year in industry.

TRAINING/WORK
EXPERIENCE

TRAINING / WORK EXPERIENCE

This section covers opportunities to undertake paid work in Britain and abroad, either as a study or career-related training placement or more simply as a period of work experience. Placements include opportunities overseas through agencies based in this country; training/work experience programmes with companies in Britain, in some cases as the first stage of a sponsorship scheme; and work experience including jobs with travel companies as a courier or campsite representative.

In preparing **A Year Between** we contacted hundreds of companies throughout Britain in order to identify opportunities for placement schemes for post-A level students. Those companies who run suitable year between placement schemes have been listed here. However, this is by no means a comprehensive guide to all the companies where placements are available; over 200 of them benefit through placements offered under the Year In Industry scheme (see page 75) and therefore although able to place students on a year between are not listed here individually. Other companies have no nationwide policy of placements; they may offer a limited number of placements but not a sufficient number, nor on a continuing basis, to be included here. In many cases such international or national companies prefer those interested to apply to their nearest regional establishment, who may have specific links with local educational establishments and offer places accordingly.

There are also companies who in the past have offered year between placements but, because of the current economic climate are currently unable to do so. However, their policy may change depending on market circumstances, and it is worthwhile considering approaching major companies on an individual basis to enquire of their current possibilities. Your school careers teacher, local careers office or Jobcentre should be able to help you identify possibilities locally.

For many a period of training during a year between will provide an invaluable transition from years of educational isolation from commercial realities to the wider world of business. One of the major benefits of any period of work experience is the placement of educational studies within the greater context of the industrial or commercial world. GEC Ferranti Defence Systems, one of the largest companies in the GEC-Marconi group, feels that in addition to this contextual benefit, an industrial placement in the year between benefits students by giving them an opportunity to find out about business life before committing themselves to a career. For other companies, such as BP, it has always been standard practice to encourage students to take a year out, as in their view it provides an opportunity to gain valuable industrial experience. The placement also benefits the companies by giving them the equivalent of an extended interview period.

Most of the major companies commit large resources to their sponsorship programme, including the opportunities in the year between, confident in the knowledge that such a programme has and will continue to provide them with senior managers. The placement also provides the students with the opportunity to assess the attractiveness of a future in that particular job/industry, and the potential benefits of the individual employer. With so much at stake, employers will go to great lengths to ensure that the industrial placement is well organised and meaningful. Many will organise specific courses to develop interpersonal, decision-making and team-building skills in addition to the period spent at the workface itself. A well-rounded placement will also include stints in other commercial areas of the organisation, such as finance, personnel, sales and marketing. Many of the industrial training opportunities should also be open to those who decide to go straight into higher education after A levels, following either a thick or thin sandwich course.

The Year In Industry offers challenging industrial experience and training in the year between, placing students to undertake real work in a company, backed by a structured programme of short courses at a college or university. The Year In Industry believes that students who have taken a year out make better informed career decisions, are more motivated on their degree course, and tend to get better degrees. The skills gained can be personal - working in a team, learning to communicate ideas, generally gaining confidence and maturity - or technical. It is generally recognised that students with this kind of experience go on to do better on their degree course. Professor R Farrar of Southampton University:

Some 50% of our students have had industrial experience before taking their course here. These students perform distinctly better than those who came staright from school.

Off the job, many companies and placing organisations like The Year In Industry also organise seminars and workshops on subjects like communication, design, finance, market and project planning.

Sanjay was accepted onto the Arthur Andersen Scholarship Programme, which offers the opportunity to gain insight into chartered accountancy, business and finance, starting with the year between. He feels he had a tremendous head start over his contemporaries:

Some of my friends have had to stack supermarket shelves in order to finance their pre-university travels. Others have

managed to gain professional experience but without the benefit of a travel grant or the encouragement to take time off to travel before university. I had the best of both worlds.

Susan was also attracted to join the Andersen Scholarship Programme before going on to read accountancy and finance at Warwick University. She had already decided to do an accountancy degree, but felt it would be useful to gain some practical experience beforehand:

To begin with the work seemed very daunting, but the training I received gave me the confidence I needed. It has been very challenging, but I have been given plenty of feedback and support. At first it was difficult to get used to doing a full day's work and then having to go home and cook, but I have now got used to it. I have learnt a lot about my own capabilities and limitations.

From the companies' point of view, they benefit from the opportunities offered to year between students by gaining initial access to future graduates and they also profit from the work undertaken. Training placements are also often the first step to obtaining sponsorship for a degree course from the employing company. However, many students on a year between feel it may be too early to commit themselves to a particular career or sphere of business. They feel that a period of work is necessary to give themselves an educational break, but the placement is seen as a way of testing the waters of business and commerce, generating some income for further years of study or offering the opportunity to put gained educational skills, such as foreign languages or mathematics, into practice.

Interspeak specialises in finding *stages* for year between students. The organisation feels that a year out is extremely beneficial, and they lay particular emphasis on the linguistic, cultural and social experience. Interspeak consider that a year out can lead to greater social mobility and a better understanding of different ways of life. However, they warn that generally the foreign language competence of British students taking a year between is far below their mainland European partners, and this will limit the greater benefits to be achieved from a placement in another country.

If you are uncertain about the commitment of a work placement, or are unable to be accepted on a particular scheme, then you may be able to find temporary paid work through employment agencies. Sometimes local authorities offer suitable short-term employment for students or school-leavers. Supermarkets also take on short-term staff, and department stores often recruit for busy sales periods (usually Christmas, January and July). The Central Bureau's annual information guide **Working Holidays** also has thousands of short-term paid work opportunities from a few weeks to several months. However you should bear in mind that time spent stacking shelves or grape picking, for example, is unlikely to improve your own self-esteem or impress future employers reading your *cv*, unless the job is to be used as a means to finance a more challenging project, such as an expedition or a period of community service on the other side of the world. If your year between is to be of real benefit you should concentrate on opportunities that will stretch your capabilities and give you new skills along with a greater sense of responsibility to society as a whole. However, don't necessarily assume that only a training placement or a period of work experience in the area of industry or business in which you will find yourself studying or finally working will be of relevance. Think laterally, use the opportunity of a year between to broaden your horizons; undertaking a work placement complementary to your future course of study can be a greater challenge and in the long term of greater value.

Arthur Andersen Chartered Accountants

Binnie & Partners Consulting Engineers

BP Research

British Universities North America Club

Canvas Holidays

Carisma Holidays

Data Connection Ltd

Eurocamp

Ford Motor Company Ltd

GAP Activity Projects (GAP) Ltd

GEC Ferranti Defence Systems Ltd

The Henley Centre for Forecasting Ltd

ICC Information Group Ltd

Interspeak Ltd

Jobs in the Alps

John Laing plc

Lucas Industries plc

Pfizer Ltd (Central Research)

PGL Young Adventure Ltd

Shell Research Ltd

Solaire International Holidays

Studentours

The Year In Industry

Youth Hostels Association

ARTHUR ANDERSEN
CHARTERED ACCOUNTANTS

National Scholarship Programme Coordinator, Arthur Andersen Chartered Accountants, 1 Surrey Street, London WC2R 2PS

071-438 3110

Ten offices throughout the UK

One of the largest firms of chartered accountants, employing over 50,000 people worldwide

Offers an opportunity for young people to gain insight into chartered accountancy, business and finance through a scholarship programme. The programme comprises a paid training and work experience programme, support during a university degree course, with further paid summer work experience and the potential offer of a full-time job as a trainee chartered accountant on graduation.

Ages 17+. UK nationals only. Applicants should anticipate gaining 3 A or B grades at A level, preferably including mathematics; GCSE grade A in mathematics also essential. Applicants should have a keen interest in business and finance. **B D PH**

Initial year out training and work experience programme lasts 35 weeks; entire scholarship programme lasts 4 years, including 6 weeks during each summer vacation. Participants are not obliged to continue with the scholarship once the course is over, nor are they made to take on a long-term commitment; it is simply hoped they will want to join the firm after graduation.

During the initial programme work is for 37½ hours per week at a rate of £7,000 per annum, plus additional pay for overtime. On completion of the programme in May there is a travel bonus of £1,500. At the beginning of each academic year participants receive £1,200 based on satisfactory performance over the previous period of work. Vacation work paid at a rate commensurate with experience.

Throughout the programme participants' performance is reviewed by the professionals for whom they are working, and during their time at university they are kept in touch with the firm's activities

Apply at the beginning of last year at school; interviews usually held during Christmas holidays

BINNIE & PARTNERS
CONSULTING ENGINEERS

 Mr M E Hannah, Director, Administration & Staff, Binnie & Partners Consulting Engineers, Grosvenor House, 69 London Road, Redhill, Surrey RH1 1LQ

Redhill (0737) 774155

Redhill

A partnership of professional engineers, with a worldwide staff of over 1,000. Involved in water supply, irrigation, energy, waste water and infrastructure engineering, the firm employs engineers in many disciplines to provide a wide range of consultancy services.

Two school leavers are recruited each year to work applying their scientific knowledge in a computer-based environment

Ages 17-19. Applicants must have, or be expecting to gain, 3 good A levels (or equivalent) in mathematics, physics and one other maths or science based subject, and intend to read for a mathematics, physics or engineering degree. An interest in computing, an enthusiastic approach to problem-solving and an ability to think laterally essential.

6-12 months, usually September-August

Participants work a 37½ hour week and earn a salary of £7,900 per annum. Accommodation provided for the first two weeks while participants look for somewhere to live.

Apply as soon as possible

BP RESEARCH

The Training Officer, BP Research, Sunbury Research Centre, Chertsey Road, Sunbury-on-Thames, Middlesex TW13 4JL

Sunbury-on-Thames (0932) 762030

Sunbury-on-Thames

Most of BP's activities centre around oil and gas, but it has also been moving into activities such as chemicals and plastics, detergents, coal, information technology, nutrition and alternative energy, as well as new ventures such as photovoltaic energy and materials for the aerospace industry. The Sunbury Research Centre provides support to existing BP industries and stimulus for the growth of new businesses.

Offers employment for those intending to study a science based course at university/ polytechnic. Participants are assigned to work in areas that, where possible, are relevant to their proposed course of study. They work as part of a project team on real issues under the guidance of an experienced team member. Most participants write a report at the end of the year which may be of use both to their future studies and to the Research Centre itself. 10-20 placements available each year.

Ages 17/18+. Applicants must be expecting to gain 3 good A levels (or equivalent), Grade C or above preferred, in science based subjects such as mathematics, physics, chemistry, computing, statistics or geology. They should have, or intend to apply for a place at university/polytechnic. **B D PH**

6+ months; 12 months preferred

Students work a 37½ hour week and receive a salary of £7,500 per annum (September 1991) plus Outer London allowance

Assessment and appraisal from training supervisor throughout the placement

Apply in the autumn of final year at school/college

BRITISH UNIVERSITIES NORTH AMERICA CLUB (BUNAC)

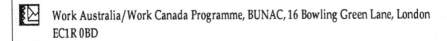 Work Australia/Work Canada Programme, BUNAC, 16 Bowling Green Lane, London EC1R 0BD

071-251 3472

Australia, Canada

A non-profitmaking, non-political, educational student club venture which aims to foster international understanding, principally through student work exchange programmes

Offers opportunities for students wishing to work and travel. Before departure, help is given with finding employment, which can include hotel, restaurant and shop work; selling ice cream, sandwiches, soft drinks and fast food; or working in a laundry or an amusement park. Alternatively, participants can opt to find a job once they have arrived in the country. Also operates short-term placements on summer camps in the United States, and summer work programmes in Jamaica and the United States.

Ages 18-25 (Australia); 18-29 (Canada). Applicants should have enthusiasm, motivation, confidence, initiative and be prepared to work hard. For the Work Canada Programme, applicants will need to have proof that they are returning to full-time education. For all programmes they must show evidence of adequate funds or sponsorship, and proof of return or round-trip transportation.

2-12 months. Workers are free to spend time after their placement travelling around the country.

Australia: participants pay £1042-£1500 (1991) to cover flight and registration fee. Canada: participants pay £55 registration fee, £356-£493 return flight, £76 insurance and £3 membership fee. All work is paid, but participants will have to find their own accommodation.

Compulsory orientation programmes held throughout Britain at Easter, and in host country on arrival, giving advice on finding and choosing a job, obtaining a visa, income tax, accommodation, travel, food and budgeting. Information also provided on onward travel.

Apply for information in November

CANVAS HOLIDAYS

 The Operations Manager, Canvas Holidays, 12 Abbey Park Place, Dunfermline

 Dunfermline (0383) 620369

 Austria, France, Germany, Italy, Spain, Switzerland

 A tour operator providing ready-erected, fully equipped tents and cabins on campsites throughout Europe

 Resident campsite couriers are required to help erect and clean out tents, check equipment, look after clients, organise activities, help with administration, and dismantle and store tents at the end of the season. Children's couriers, nannies and watersports instructors are also needed on some sites. Also require applicants to form flying squads, teams of 2-3 people who help set up and dismantle 200-250 tents in approx 12 campsites; sometimes they can continue working as resident campsite couriers. Recruits some 360 couriers each year.

 Ages 18-25 (21-25 for flying squad members). UK nationals only. Applicants should be sociable, enthusiastic, practical, reliable, self-motivated, able to turn their hand to new and varied tasks, and have a sense of humour. Flying squad members need to be fit and able to work long hours under pressure without supervision, and cope with living out of a rucksack. Children's couriers, nannies and watersports instructors should have relevant experience/qualifications. Knowledge of relevant language essential for resident couriers, desirable for flying squad members. Valid international driving licence an advantage.

 6 months, April-October

 No fixed hours, as workload varies from day to day and is especially busy at beginning and end of season. Transport to site provided; return travel dependent on completion of contract. Salary £76 per week (1991); insurance, accommodation in frame tents and moped/bicycle for use on site provided.

 Apply at any time; interviews commence early November for following season

CARISMA HOLIDAYS

The Operations Manager, Carisma Holidays, Bethel House, Heronsgate Road, Chorleywood, Hertfordshire WD3 5BB

Chorleywood (0923) 284235

France

A family-run business organising holidays in tents and mobile homes on beach sites along the Atlantic coast of France, from Brittany to Biarritz

Recruits approx 25 resident couriers each year. Work involves welcoming families, providing information and advice, cleaning and maintaining tents and mobile homes, and babysitting for clients when necessary.

Ages 17+. Applicants should have a helpful and friendly disposition and experience of dealing with people. Good spoken French and English essential.

2-5 months, beginning early May or late June

Salary £60-£75 per week, depending on experience and level of responsibility. Self-catering accommodation provided on site in tents or mobile homes. Travel costs paid.

Full training given on site at start of season

Apply as early as possible

DATA CONNECTION LTD

 The Recruitment Administrator, Data Connection Ltd, 100 Church Street, Enfield, Middlesex EN2 6BQ

 081-366 1177

 Enfield

 A computer software engineering company founded in 1981, with a reputation for developing complex, high quality software to tight deadlines. Specialises in communications, retail point of sale and graphics.

 Employs a number of pre-university and vacation students each year to give them practical paid experience in software engineering. Students are assigned significant pieces of work to do as part of a small project team. They work within the limits of their knowledge, and are given lots of help. Awards university sponsorship to outstanding students who then return for a minimum of 8 weeks during each summer vacation. There is no obligation for sponsorship students to join Data Connection after graduation.

 Ages 17-20. No previous experience necessary, but versatility and creativity, the ability to communicate ideas, energy, enthusiasm and an aptitude to learn programming are desirable. Applicants should have at least 3 A levels (or equivalent) at A or B grades in numerate subjects.

 3-12 months, 8-9 weeks for vacation placements

 Students work a 37½ hour week and receive approx £600 per month. Self-catering accommodation provided locally in a large house shared with other students.

 Review at end of placement

 Recruitment all year

EUROCAMP

Courier Department, Eurocamp, Edmundson House, Tatton Street, Knutsford, Cheshire WA16 6BG

Knutsford (0565) 650052

Austria, Belgium, France, Germany, Italy, Spain, Switzerland

Organises self-drive holidays providing fully equipped tents and caravans on campsites throughout Europe

Resident couriers are required to clean and maintain tents and equipment, replenish gas supplies, keep the store tent in order, keep accounts and report back to England. They also meet holidaymakers on arrival, organise activities, provide information on local events and attractions and sort out any problems they may have. At the beginning and end of the season they help erect and dismantle tents.

Ages 18+. Applicants should be familiar with working and travelling abroad, preferably with some camping experience. They should also be adaptable, reliable, independent, efficient, hardworking, sensible, sociable, tactful, patient and have a working knowledge of the relevant language.

3 or 6 months, beginning April or July.

No set working hours or free days, as these depend on unpredictable factors. Salary £88 per week. Accommodation provided in tents with cooking facilities, plus insurance, return travel and moped/bicycle for use on site.

Training provided

Apply as early as possible; interviews start September/October

FORD MOTOR COMPANY LTD

Senior Training Officer (ESP), College Recruitment & Education Liaison, Room 1/360, Ford Motor Company Ltd, Eagle Way, Brentwood, Essex CM13 3BW

England, Wales, Northern Ireland

Established in the UK since 1911, Ford is one of Britain's largest manufacturing concerns with plants producing cars and commercial vehicles throughout England, Wales and Northern Ireland, employing some 43,000 people

Operates a sponsorship scheme combining industrial training with support during a degree course. Students carry out key engineering assignments which benefit both their own and corporate objectives. 60 places are available each year.

Ages 17/18+. Applicants should have good GCSEs and relevant A levels, and must plan to take a degree course in mechanical, electrical/electronic, automotive, manufacturing or production engineering at an institution approved by Ford. **PH**

Students work a minimum of 18 months during their sponsorship period. Those doing a pre-university year with Ford are therefore required to do two further 3 month placements during summer vacations.

During placements students work 37½ hours per week and are paid a salary related to the year of their course, starting from £790 per month. Tax free bursaries are paid during each academic year. There is no legal obligation to join Ford on graduating, neither is there any guarantee that a job will be offered; currently approx 60% of sponsored students join Ford as graduates.

Students attend a 3 day induction course, followed by a 5 day personal development course at beginning of placement. Formal performance appraisal is carried out every three months.

Applicants should first apply for a place on an approved degree course, then apply to Ford before the end of January during their last year at school

GAP ACTIVITY PROJECTS (GAP) LTD

The Company Secretary, GAP House, 44 Queen's Road, Reading, Berkshire RG1 4BB

Canada, France, Germany

A charity founded in 1972 to give those with a year between leaving school and going on to further/higher education or vocational training the opportunity to work in another country

A few business placements are available in offices, banks, supermarkets and factories. Work is mainly as office juniors or general assistants.

Ages 18-19. UK nationals only. Applicants should be reliable, possess initiative and intelligence, and be prepared to work hard. Those working on French or German projects must be able to speak the relevant language.

2-9 months

Board, accommodation and salary provided. Participants must find their own travel and insurance costs, plus the placement fee of £150-£300, depending on country chosen.

Candidates attend a briefing session before departure

Apply early in September of last year at school; interviews held November-March

GEC FERRANTI DEFENCE SYSTEMS LTD

Brian Gillon, Graduate Education Adviser, GEC Ferranti Defence Systems Ltd, St Andrews Works, Robertson Avenue, Edinburgh EH11 1PX

031-337 2442

Edinburgh

One of the largest companies in the GEC-Marconi Group, combining Ferranti Defence Systems with the airborne radar interests of GEC-Marconi and the business of Marconi Test Systems. It has four main trading divisions: Radar Systems, Display Systems, Navigation Systems and Logistic Systems.

Offers paid industrial and commercial placements at pre-university and undergraduate level, involving on- and off-the-job training in both technical and commercial areas. Some 80 placements available each year, mainly in engineering/science.

Ages 18+. Applicants should have high A level (or equivalent) grades and be intending to take a degree in electrical, electronic, mechanical or production engineering, physics or computer science. Undergraduates should be aiming for a 2nd class honours degree in any of these subjects.

Pre-university: 3 months, beginning June; or 12 months, beginning September. Undergraduate: 3 months, beginning June; 6 months, beginning April; or 12 months, beginning September.

Trainees work a 37½ hour week and receive a salary of £100 per week (pre-university) or £141 per week (undergraduates). They must find and pay for their own board and lodging. Subsidised canteen available.

Placement supervisors complete a training placement appraisal, which the trainees see and sign

Apply before the end of December

THE HENLEY CENTRE FOR FORECASTING LTD

The Office Manager, Henley Centre for Forecasting, 2 Tudor Street, Blackfriars, London EC4Y 0AA

071-353 9961

London

The Henley Centre relies on the work of its economists, demographers, social scientists and specialists to deliver to its clients an accurate evaluation of all factors influencing the size, performance and direction of their markets. Clients then use this intelligence to plan and devise products tuned to the desires of the consumer.

Recruits 3 assistants annually to help with research and the preparation of data. As it is a relatively small company participants are able to benefit from getting to know how all the various departments work and inter-relate.

Ages 17-21. Applicants should be keen, enthusiastic and eager to learn. No previous experience necessary. Applicants should have A level or equivalent qualifications, and excellent English skills.

9-11 months

Participants work a 35 hour week and receive a salary of approx £8,500 per annum

Apply as early as possible, places are limited

ICC INFORMATION GROUP LTD

Human Resources Director, ICC Information Group Ltd, 72 Oldfield Road, Hampton, Middlesex TW12 2HQ

081-783 0350

Hampton, central London and Cardiff

Established in 1969, ICC provides market and financial information to the business sector.

Offers 5-10 one-year placements for undergraduates. Work is available in the fields of market research, data analysis, property search, sales support and editorial.

Ages 20-25. All nationalities accepted; good English essential. No special experience or qualifications required. Applicants should be highly motivated with good business and commercial sense. PH

12 months minimum

Employees work 35-40 hours per week in return for wages at the going rate. They are responsible for finding their own accommodation.

Recruitment all year

INTERSPEAK LTD

 David Ratcliffe, Managing Director, Interspeak Ltd, The Coach House, Blackwood Estate, Blackwood, Lanarkshire ML11 0JG

 Lanark (0555) 894219

 Mainly the UK and France; possibly Spain, Italy, Germany and the United States

 Specialises in finding quality *stages* in the UK for students from mainland Europe who have a good level of spoken and written English, and can also find some placements abroad for UK students.

 Placements are available in the fields of marketing, international trade, secretarial, computing, engineering, hotel and catering, and in schools. Places up to 1,000 students each year in the UK and abroad.

 Ages 18-29. Applicants should have an enquiring and open mind, and an interest in the world of business and commerce. Initiative and commonsense are key attributes, as is the ability to work as part of a team. Applicants should have at least A level qualifications or equivalent; school leavers should be planning to go on to further or higher education. Previous work experience is highly desirable, and an excellent written and spoken level of the relevant language is absolutely essential. **B D PH**

 6-12 months

 Participants work 30-40 hours a week; salary varies depending on employer. In order to maximise the linguistic, social and cultural benefit to participants accommodation is in host families; cost £90-£125 per week. Insurance is provided, but participants pay their own travel costs. Booking fee £150-£330 depending on length of placement and how far in advance application is made.

 Participants on industrial/commercial placements may attend an orientation course; average cost £300 per week. Individual monitoring takes place throughout the placement, and participants are encouraged to prepare a short report.

 Apply at least 2 months in advance

JOBS IN THE ALPS

Jobs in the Alps Agency, PO Box 388, London SW1X 8LX

France, Germany, Switzerland

Established in 1972, Jobs in the Alps can place young people in Swiss alpine resort hotels, and carries out aptitude tests on behalf of hotels in France and Germany

The work is mainly as hall or night porters, waiting staff, receptionists, barmaids, chambermaids or kitchen helpers, in hotels with an international clientèle

Ages 18+. Good knowledge of French or German required for the more interesting jobs. Applicants must be prepared to work hard and to a high professional standard, alongside an international workforce.

3-4 months, beginning December or June

Employees work 8-9 hours each day, with 1-2 days free per week. Pay approx £80-£110 per week; board, lodging and insurance provided. £25 service charge and £10 per month fee depending on length of contract for placements in Switzerland; subscription fee to JITA Club required for placements in France or Germany. Interview fee £1.

Apply by 30 September for winter placements; by 30 March for summer placements

JOHN LAING PLC

Career Development Manager, John Laing plc, Page Street, Mill Hill, London NW7 2ER

081-906 5243

Throughout the UK

One of Britain's largest construction and civil engineering groups, working in the research, development, design and manufacturing of products for the building industry

Offers work at construction sites and offices to students wishing to embark on a career in the construction industry. A few opportunities available for students to work for a year prior to sponsorship on a degree course; generally only a few of the students sponsored opt for a year out before their degree. The benefits are that it can help candidates decide that they have made the right career choice; the major drawback is that of returning to academic life after a year as a wage-earner. Also run a sixth form project each year in October, where participants work for a week designing, planning, evaluating and constructing a footbridge.

Ages 16-19. UK nationals only. Applicants should have an interest in the construction industry and evidence that they have what it takes to work in this challenging environment. Previous experience not essential.

Usually 3 months, or 12 months for year out placements

Participants work a 40 hour week, with salary and employers' public liability insurance provided

Apply as soon as possible

LUCAS INDUSTRIES PLC

Manager, Graduate Recruitment & Development, Lucas Industries plc, Great King Street, Birmingham B19 2XF

021-554 5252

Sites throughout the UK

A major international company and a world leader in the design and manufacture of high-technology products supplied to aerospace, automotive and industrial markets. Lucas consider taking a year out broadens a person's experience and vision and is therefore beneficial.

Offers paid engineering placements. Places up to 20 school leavers each year.

Ages 18+. EC nationals only. Applicants must have a desire to work in industry, plan to take a degree in engineering, and have appropriate A levels or equivalent. **B D PH**

3-12 months

Participants work approx 40 hours per week for a paid salary. Insurance cover on site.

PFIZER LTD (CENTRAL RESEARCH)

Personnel Officer, Pfizer Ltd (Central Research), Ramsgate Road, Sandwich, Kent CT13 9NJ

Sandwich (0304) 618719

Sandwich

An international research-based company established in New York in 1849 and concerned with the development and manufacture of pharmaceuticals. Most of Pfizer's business is in health care, but the company also operates in the fields of agriculture, speciality chemicals, materials science and consumer products. Some 3,000 people around the world are employed in Pfizer's research centres, and the Sandwich centre is the second largest in the group.

Work placements are available in data management, helping to set up and maintain databases, reviewing and inputting data from clinical trials. Occasionally work is also available in chemistry or biology research laboratories. 3-6 placements are offered each year.

Ages 17/18+. Applicants must have relevant A levels, such as mathematics, statistics or computer studies, or appropriate science subject for work in laboratories. They should be well-motivated, with an interest in pharmaceutical research and development. **PH**

6-12 months

Trainees work a 37 hour week in return for a salary of £7,255 per annum (1991). Help can be given with finding accommodation.

In-company induction held

Recruitment all year

PGL YOUNG ADVENTURE LTD

Personnel Manager, PGL Young Adventure Ltd, Alton Court, Penyard Lane (878), Ross-on-Wye, Herefordshire HR9 5NR

Ross-on-Wye (0989) 764211

Throughout Britain and France

Organises activity holidays for young people and families, and self-catering holidays on campsites

Positions are available for activity instructors and support staff, including kitchen/domestic assistants, cooks, sites assistants, stores organisers, drivers and administration assistants. Also more senior posts such as couriers, group leaders, TEFL teachers and supervisors. Approx 2,000 young people work for PGL each year.

Ages 18+ (20+ for work abroad and for more senior positions). Applicants must have plenty of energy, enthusiasm and a good sense of humour. They must enjoy working in a team and be able to work and play hard. Qualifications in outdoor activities an advantage, and experience of working with children essential.

4/6+ weeks preferred. Work is available February-November.

Salary from £30 per week, depending on position. Full board and accommodation provided on site. Medical insurance cover provided, and travel from port of exit for staff working abroad.

Full training is provided for all staff, including the opportunity to take BCU, RYA, St John's Ambulance and other recognised qualifications

Apply December-April. Applicants available in May and early June have a greater chance of selection

SHELL RESEARCH LTD

Personnel Division, Shell Research Ltd, Thornton Research Centre, PO Box 1, Chester CH1 3SH

051-373 5000

Thornton Research Centre, near Chester

One of the major Shell Research and Development Centres, employing over 600 people with a wide range of scientific skills. Much of the work is concerned with the development of products such as fuels, lubricants and bitumen and the additives that go into them. The Centre also studies methods of storing and distributing petroleum products, provides advice on design and durability of equipment in hostile environments, and has a large fund of expertise in combustion science. The Centre see the year out as beneficial both to the company and to the student. The company achieves completed projects and the student learns skills, improves competencies, matures, communicates and acquires some savings before starting university.

Placements are available for approx 8 school-leavers each year who intend to read science or engineering at university

Ages 17-20. Applicants need to be keen and self-motivated and must have above average A level (or equivalent) passes in mathematics, physics and chemistry.

6-12 months, beginning September

Students work a 37½ hour week and receive a salary of £7,515 per annum. They are responsible for finding their own accommodation and pay their own travel costs.

Compulsory safety induction course organised, and an exit interview takes place at the end of the placement.

Apply as early as possible, places are limited

SOLAIRE INTERNATIONAL HOLIDAYS

Personnel Manager, Solaire International Holidays, 1158 Stratford Road, Hall Green, Birmingham B28 8AF

021-778 5061

France and Spain

A family-run company organising camping and mobile home holidays at sites on the Atlantic coast and Mediterranean in France, and on the Costa Dorada in Spain

Couriers are required to prepare tents and mobile homes at the beginning of each season, ensure the smooth running of the camps, undertake maintenance work and look after campers, and close down at the end of the season

Ages 18+. No previous experience necessary. Knowledge of French or Spanish preferable but not essential. Experience of working with children useful.

6 months, May-October

Due to the nature of the job there are no fixed hours of work. Salary £45-£70 per week; accommodation provided in tents or mobile homes on site. Insurance and travel expenses provided.

Apply before the end of the year prior to appointment

STUDENTOURS

The Director, Studentours, 3 Harcourt Street, London W1H 1DS

071-402 5131

Kent and Sussex

Founded in 1965, Studentours runs two residential leisure and learning centres in Kent and Sussex for young overseas visitors

Staff are required for various duties including organising sports programmes, supervising children's activities, helping on children's farms, domestic work, maintenance of nature study trails and an assault course, gardening, restoring Victorian architecture and the Italian gardens.

Ages 17+. No previous experience necessary.

2-6 months, all year

5+ hour day, 5 day week with evenings free. Pocket money from £40 per week. Accommodation, insurance and meals whilst on duty provided. At other times workers are provided with food but must do their own cooking.

Recruitment all year

THE YEAR IN INDUSTRY

 Brian L Tripp, National Director, The Year In Industry, University of Manchester, Simon Building, Oxford Road, Manchester M13 9PL

 061-275 4396

 Throughout the UK

 INDEX (INDustrial EXperience) and PFUE (Pre Formation of Undergraduate Engineers), two leading organisations in the field of recruiting and placing pre-university students, have joined forces to offer young people challenging industrial experience and training in the year before they start their degree

 Students do real work in a company, backed by a structured programme of short courses at a college or university to develop practical skills and business awareness. Placements are found for some 200+ trainees annually. Some students obtain sponsorship for their degree course from their employing company.

 Ages 18-19 (immediately post-A level/BTEC or equivalent). Applicants should be interested in taking up a career in industry or in finding out more about industry, and keen to gain additional personal development. They must have met entry requirements for a degree course (in any discipline) and have a confirmed offer of a place. B D PH depending on company

 11 months, September-July

 Conditions of work depend on company; typically students work 35-37½ hours per week and receive a minimum salary of £120 per week. They are responsible for finding their own accommodation.

 Compulsory induction course organised before placement, plus 20-25 days of off-the-job short courses, and continuous assessment and appraisal during placement. Students are asked to complete a special project which will be presented at the end of the year.

 Apply as soon as possible

YOUTH HOSTELS ASSOCIATION

Youth Hostels Association (England and Wales), National Office, Trevelyan House, 8 St Stephen's Hill, St Albans, Hertfordshire, AL1 2DY

St Albans (0727) 55215

Throughout England and Wales

The YHA aims to help all, especially young people of limited means, to achieve a greater knowledge, love and care of the countryside, in particular by providing hostels or other simple accommodation

Recruits assistant wardens to work at youth hostels throughout England and Wales. Work involves domestic and catering duties, helping to manage the hostel, reception work and other general duties including shopping, cleaning, serving in the shop, bookwork and maintenance. Applications and requests for further details should be made to the Regional Office of the area in which you wish to work: Wales Tel Cardiff (0222) 396766; Northern Tel 091-284 2101; Central Tel Matlock (0629); Southern Tel Salisbury (0722) 337515.

Ages 18+. No experience necessary; applicants should have a cheerful, outgoing personality. An interest in the countryside and in the work of the YHA is also desirable.

2-6 months, all year; peak periods March-September. Preference given to applicants prepared to work for most of a season.

Assistant wardens work a 5 day week, with 2 days off or payment/time in lieu. Salary £55-£60 per week, depending on location; full board accommodation and insurance provided. Applicants pay their own travel expenses.

Recruitment all year

DISCOVERY / LEADERSHIP

This section covers those organisations who can offer you the chance to learn new skills and develop ones you already have in the context of an expedition, usually to some remote corner of the world, designed to test and stretch the abilities of participants. Also covered are the short-service schemes run by the Armed Forces, which provide the opportunity to train and join a unit, develop leadership skills, and possibly travel overseas.

Expedition programmes generally involve an aspect of community service or environmental research, giving participants an awareness of the problems faced by local communities and the natural world, and the opportunity to work in some small way towards resolving them. In this way topics covered in school geography and biology lessons can become realities. And as a result of the challenges they present to participants' endurance and problem-solving abilities, many of the expeditions covered here qualify participants for Duke of Edinburgh awards.

Groups are supervised by fully trained and experienced leaders, and will tend to be made up of young people from different backgrounds. Once they are thrown together far from home, perhaps in a hostile environment, a spirit of companionship, loyalty and teamwork develops, as each participant depends on the others for the success of the project. Learning to survive in an arctic climate or jungle terrain, taking responsibility for actions which will affect other members of the group, overcoming physical hardships and tackling practical problems, all these aspects of expeditions go to develop participants' self-confidence, maturity and leadership ability.

Although leadership experience, scientific knowledge and outdoor pursuits skills are obviously very valuable qualities for potential expedition members, they are not necessarily the first things that the organisers are looking for. They will usually want a broad range of people to make up a group, and qualities such as a sense of humour, enthusiasm, determination and common sense are the most likely to help a group gel. Physical fitness is important, but you don't have to be an Olympic athlete. Many organisations encourage applications from people with disabilities, visual or hearing impairments. Above all, it is having the right motivation that counts.

For most expeditionary projects, you will be required to raise the finances to fund your participation. In some cases this is considered to be part of the challenge of joining an expedition, and participants are usually discouraged from depending on their parents' generosity, or may be asked to help out participants who have not benefited from the same advantages as them. Help and advice on fundraising is usually given, but participants are expected to rely on their own resourcefulness and imagination.

Frontier is the expeditionary arm of the Society for Environmental Exploration, established in the belief that volunteers can assist with practical solutions to some of the world's environmental problems. On its projects in Africa many of the volunteers are students taking a year out. Frontier believes that what they learn about Africa and living and working with other people significantly matures their outlook, and prepares them well for university life. Rachel McCaffery was one such volunteer, on an expedition to Tanzania in 1990:

I had to raise a lot of money to take part, but I definitely feel I got my money's worth. I made a lot of friends, managed to write a thesis on the work I did while there and it gave me a new perspective on the Third World - actually seeing it in real life rather than just news stories.

The International Scientific Support Trust's expeditionary arm, Trekforce Expeditions provides physical and logical assistance to scientists undertaking biogeographical and ecological research, as well as giving participants an opportunity for adventure and exploration in remote areas of Indonesia. Trekforce feels that taking a year out is very beneficial, as long as the year is used sensibly, and that expeditions exert a maturing influence on school leavers. Josie Kirby was a Trekforce expeditioneer:

I paid quite a large fee, but feel that it was worth every penny. I thought the expedition was excellent; meeting new peeople, working together and learning survival skills as well as actually contributing toward scientific research. It was an experience I won't forget.

The expedition programmes demand a lot from the participants, but give a lot in return. If you are concerned that your scientific, sport or physical skills may not come up to standards required, take heart from Teresa Fenoughty who interviews applicants for the British Schools Exploring Society. She stresses that at the outset of the expedition they are not necessarily looking for the winners in life:

They don't have to be the toughest rock rats. We pick students who have a real interest and potential, who might give a lot or even gain a lot from such an experience, either because they are under-confident, arrogant or immature.

The British Schools Exploring Society's expeditions create the challenge of adventure in remote environments, fostering dedication, companionship and personal initiative. The majority of destinations are Arctic/sub-Arctic environments such as Greenland, Iceland and Alaska. Lucy Wright appreciated the challenges the environment imposed on her expedition:

I've become more tolerant since the trip. Under survival conditions you have to look after those around you and take responsibility for the community. Your mistake could mean a fatal accident.

Mark Mullen joined the 2nd King Edward VII's Own Gurkha Rifles in Brunei under the Army Short Service Limited Commission (SSLC) scheme before taking up his place at London University:

Having completed a basic Nepali language course, I returned to the battalion to become platoon commander, under the watchful eye of the platoon sergeant who was always on hand to offer that vital piece of advice. Though often tired and hot in the jungle, I found it one of the most exciting and interesting environments I have ever been in. The experience of serving a SSLC has taught me a lot about myself and others. I feel my confidence has grown and my horizons have been broadened from that of a schoolboy.

Jennifer Clee also undertook an Army Short Service Commission in her year between before going on to Nottingham University:

Having passed the selection I arrived at Sandhurst for the three week course very apprehensive, and with no idea of what to expect ... my time spend there was probably the hardest, most challenging and the most rewarding of my life.

When I arrived at 28 (British) Signal regiment, part of the Northern Army Group in Germany, I was whisked straight off on a NATO exercise for ten days. Upon arriving back at camp I became 2IC of a troop, enabling me to see the role of a troop commander, and later with a little help to fulfil that role. However the Army does not believe in all work and no play, so whilst with the unit I took the rounders team to the championships in Berlin. I was also a member of the winning women's shooting team as well as representing the regiment at swimming. I managed to fit in some adventure training in the Mosel: canoeing, swimming, cycling and walking, plus some compulsory wine tasting!

Before taking up his place at Brunel University Paul Hayhurst served his Commission in Hong Kong and Hawaii with the 1st Battalion The Royal Regiment of Wales:

In Exercise Union Pacific, B Company, of which I was a member, went over to Hawaii for seven weeks to exercise with the United States Marine Corps and the US Army. This was by far the most beneficial part of my SSLC ... we were taught the principles and tactics behind a beach assault and then did a night time main assault with the Americans acting as enemy, an experience that not many British officers can boast. The Exercise also gave me an opportunity to see another country and we had sufficient time off to get out and about. I managed to go big game fishing, diving and to visit a lava flow.

Most of my time however was spent in Hong Kong. It was here that I learnt how the battalion ran and had the opportunity to carry out Orderly Officer duties. It was a very valuable experience and I had a wide variety of challenges to sort out, from compassionate cases to domestic and disciplinary problems. In Hong Kong there was also an excellent opportunity for adventure training, from waterskiing to abseiling. There were also a lot of sports played in the battalion which I was strongly encouraged to take part in, such as rugby, water polo, boxing, football and many more.

The Army Short Service Limited Commission

Brathay Exploration Group

British Schools Exploring Society

Frontier

Operation Raleigh

Royal Marines Short Service Limited Commission

TrekForce Expeditions

World Challenge Expeditions Ltd

THE ARMY SHORT SERVICE LIMITED COMMISSION

The Army Short Service Limited Commission, DAR 1d, Ministry of Defence, Room 1125, Empress State Building, Lillie Road, London SW6 1TR

UK and overseas

Aims to give young men and women a unique opportunity to develop their self-confidence and maturity in the testing environment of a front-line unit. In return, the Army gains the services of a number of young officers who make an important contribution to the life of their units, and who, it is hoped, will carry a favourable impression of their Army service into their later careers.

Open to young men and women with time between leaving school and going to university or polytechnic. SSLC officers serve as second lieutenants in Regular Army units, where possible overseas, but not on active-service operations. Recruits 40-60 SSLC officers annually.

Ages 18-20. The most successful candidates are of high academic ability who have usually been prefects or leading members of school societies or sports teams. They should have wide interests with a taste for outdoor pursuits and a sense of adventure. UK nationals only. Applicants must have a confirmed place at a UK university or polytechnic to read for a recognised degree, with all academic work and examinations completed commencing the placement.

4-18 months, beginning October and March

SSLC officers receive a salary of £8,824 per annum, from which they pay for board and lodging. They live in their own study bedroom in the officers' mess, with all meals provided. Hours vary depending on the work of the unit where officers are placed. Travel costs provided.

All applicants must attend a 4 day selection at the Regular Commissions Board in Westbury, Wiltshire. Successful candidates then attend a 3 week course at the Royal Military Academy, Sandhurst. SSLC officers receive a report from their commanding officer at the end of their tour.

Applications should be made through careers teachers to local Army Schools Liaison Officers. Recruitment all year.

BRATHAY EXPLORATION GROUP

The Administrator, Brathay Exploration Group, Brathay Hall, Ambleside, Cumbria LA22 0HP

Ambleside (053 94) 33942

UK and worldwide

Established in the 1950s, BEG is a non-profitmaking, voluntary organisation running expeditions aimed at increasing members' understanding of the natural environment, people and cultures of the places visited

Applicants are invited to become members of expeditions, usually exploring wild, rugged, remote or mountainous areas. Members have the opportunity to develop outdoor skills, carry out scientific surveys or take part in conservation tasks. Expeditions planned for 1992 include monitoring numbers of eider duck and shag on the Shetland Island of Foula; cycling around the western corner of Iceland; carrying out urban and rural surveys in southern China; and following the famous Tour de Mont Blanc route through the French, Swiss and Italian Alps.

Ages 15-30. Most expeditions require applicants with a good level of fitness and some experience of outdoor pursuits. PH

1-4 weeks, April-September

Members pay an expedition fee which covers all travel from a specified meeting point, food and accommodation (usually in tents), scientific and camping equipment, and insurance. Bursary funds are available, as is advice on raising funds for those who may have difficulty raising the expedition fee.

Training weekends held. Expedition members are generally given training on the spot with any special skills such as snow and ice work or climbing techniques.

Early application advised; expeditions are popular

BRITISH SCHOOLS EXPLORING SOCIETY

The Executive Director, British Schools Exploring Society, Royal Geographical Society, 1 Kensington Gore, London SW7 2AR

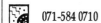

071-584 0710

Generally Arctic/sub-Arctic environments such as Greenland, Iceland, Spitzbergen, Norway, Canada and Alaska; although destinations have also included Botswana, India, Kenya and Papua New Guinea

Founded in 1932 by the late Surgeon Commander G Murray Levick, a member of Scott's 1910 Antarctic Expedition, the Society provides opportunities for young people to take part in exploratory projects led by experts from the universities, teaching and medical professions, industry and the Services. Expeditions create the challenge of adventure in remote environments, fostering dedication, companionship and personal initiative.

Expeditions planned include radio-tracking Arctic foxes in the Svarlbad archipelago of Arctic Norway; glaciological work, including the study of dust storms, on Iceland's Sylgjujokull glacier; and paddling in kayaks and carrying out a life science programme on the White Sea of Russia. Each expedition has approx 24 participants (72 on summer trips) grouped into teams of 10-15 travelling and working together on specific tasks.

Ages 16½-19. Applicants should be keen on taking up the challenges offered by harsh and hostile environments, interested in the natural world and related science projects, and willing to work as part of a small team. They must have some knowledge of camping and hillwalking, although specialised mountaineering skills are not essential. An ability in natural/life sciences is also desirable. **D PH** but full walking ability essential

3-4 months, usually beginning in spring; or 6 weeks, mid July-late August

Participants are expected to contribute equally to the costs of the expedition, from £1,500-£3,000 depending on destination and length. Costs cover return travel, freight, food, insurance and equipment. Advice and assistance is given with fundraising, considered to be part of the challenge, involving participants' drive and initiative.

Participants are issued with expedition handbooks and attend informal get-togethers, plus at least one training weekend. Each expedition makes an audio-visual presentation in January, and reports are published in the Society's *Annual Report* in June.

Apply as soon as possible for 3/4 month expeditions - selection weekends held in late autumn. Apply by 31 October for 6 week summer programmes.

FRONTIER

 Frontier, Studio 210, Thames House, 566 Cable Street, London E1 9HB

 071-790 4424

 East Africa: Tanzania and Uganda

 Expeditionary arm of the Society for Environmental Exploration, established in 1989 in the belief that volunteers can assist with practical solutions to some of the world's environmental problems. Expeditions carry out priority research and conservation projects identified by governments, scientists and research institutions of collaborating countries, and provide support for international research workers.

 Volunteers work with fellow recruits under the direction of research scientists in the setting up of specific projects. In general the work is basic scientific research or more manual labour such as construction work. Examples of projects include monitoring tidal currents in a mangrove delta; setting up underwater tourist diving trails on a coral reef; or studying chimpanzees in a forest reserve. Recruits approx 200 volunteers each year.

 Ages 17-30. Expeditions are often in remote, inaccessible and inhospitable environments, so volunteers must be capable of operating efficiently under difficult circumstances. A high value is placed on enthusiasm, tolerance, willingness to learn and an interest in environmental and development issues. Scientific qualifications and experience not essential.

 3 months, beginning January, April, July and October. Each expedition lasts 10 weeks, but air tickets are valid for slightly longer, allowing volunteers to travel independently after work has finished.

 Relies largely on contributions from volunteers to run the expedition; these amount to £2,400 for 3 months including return flight, medical insurance, vehicles, equipment, food and fuel. Some advice given on raising funds. Living conditions are basic, with accommodation under canvas and simple food. Volunteers generally work 40-50 hours per week.

 Recruitment all year

OPERATION RALEIGH

Venturer Division, Operation Raleigh, The Powerhouse, Alpha Place, Flood Street, London SW3 5SZ

071-351 7541

Worldwide

Operation Raleigh is a charity running a series of expeditions across the world for people from many nations. It aims to provide a unique opportunity for young people to develop their self-confidence and leadership skills by stretching themselves mentally and physically whilst at the same time helping others.

Venturers join expeditions based on community work, scientific research and conservation, with a strong ingredient of adventure. Expeditions consist of some 120 venturers split into groups of 5-15 to tackle individual projects, which may include improving primary health care; constructing schools, bridges, and water supplies; studying the effects of pollution on ecology; or gathering information for scientific surveys. Adventure projects are an essential feature of expeditions: venturers go trekking deserts, climbing glaciers and exploring little known corners of the earth.

Ages 17-25. No formal qualifications necessary. Applicants must understand basic English and be able to swim 500 metres. An intensive selection process is held to discover those with the motivation, determination, compatibility and humour to cope with the demands of expedition life. Evidence of leadership ability and a genuine commitment to help others also required. **B D PH**

10 weeks

Non-returnable registration fee of £5. Once selected, each Venturer is asked to raise £2,750 to cover the cost of their participation, including travel and insurance. Advice and support is given on fundraising. 150 places available each year through a Youth Development Programme for young people from disadvantaged backgrounds.

Selection tests take place over a weekend and are tough, challenging and rewarding. Those on the Youth Development Programme receive a week's special pre-expedition training.

Recruitment all year

ROYAL MARINES SHORT SERVICE LIMITED COMMISSION

Royal Marines Short Service Limited Commission, SO2(R), DCGRM, Old Admiralty Building, Spring Gardens, London SW1A 2BE

UK and possibly overseas

The Royal Marines are the Royal Navy's soldiers and Britain's commandos; a tightly-knit corps of highly trained men led by officers worthy of a tradition of resolute and positive command. Their principal role nowadays is the defence of the northern flank of Europe in the NATO alliance, bridging the gap between land and sea warfare.

The SSLC is specifically designed to cater for those taking a year between school and university or polytechnic, allowing some 20 men each year the chance to experience the life of a Royal Marines officer. Officers gain in leadership ability, responsibility and fitness, and learn a number of skills reflecting the need for adaptability.

Male UK nationals only. Candidates must have a confirmed place at a UK university or polytechnic to read for a recognised degree, and be under 22 years in September of the year of entry to higher education. Successful candidates are those with leadership qualities such as physical fitness, intelligence, mental ability, a sense of humour and the ability to communicate effectively. They are likely to have been prefects or leading members of school societies or sports teams, and should have wide interests with a taste for outdoor pursuits and a sense of adventure.

9 months, beginning October

SSLC Officers receive a salary of £6,249 per annum, from which a small charge is made for food and accommodation. They have their own single room in the officers' mess. A uniform is issued free, limited to those items required during the 9 months' service. Travel costs are provided where necessary. There is leave entitlement at Easter and in the summer, and a further two weeks' leave before going on to higher education.

All candidates attend a 2½ day Potential Officers Course at the Commando Training Centre Royal Marines and the Admiralty Interview Board before they can be considered for a commission. Results of the selection process are made known to candidates by late August. The first three weeks of the commission consist of an intensive training period. A full report from the commanding officer is given at the end of the commission.

Apply before the end of April. Further information and application forms can also be obtained from Royal Navy or Royal Marines Liaison Officers.

TREKFORCE EXPEDITIONS

Wandy Swales, Chief Executive, Trekforce Expeditions, International Scientific Support Trust Ltd, 58 Battersea Park Road, London SW11 4JP

071-498 0855

Indonesia

Expeditionary arm of the International Scientific Support Trust, a non-profitmaking company founded in 1990; charitable status applied for. Expeditions provide physical and logistical assistance to scientists undertaking biogeographical and ecological research, as well as giving participants an opportunity for adventure and exploration in remote areas of Indonesia.

Projects in 1991 included studying the ecology of grasshoppers and the altitudinal zoning of rainforests on Sulawesi. For 1992 scientific expeditions are planned to Irian Jaya, Sumatra and the Talaud Islands, as well as a challenge trek through Java, Bali and Lombok.

Ages 18+. Applicants should be good mixers, enthusiastic, energetic and keen on the outdoor life. No experience necessary. All nationalities welcome, but good English essential. All applicants must be able to swim. B D

6 weeks-6 months, June-November. Each expedition lasts 6 weeks, and participants may opt for 2 weeks of independent travel after initial expedition.

Cost from £2,250 for 6 weeks includes return flight, insurance, food, jungle accommodation, guides, ground transport and training. Some advice is given to participants about raising funds.

Participants undergo 4 days of jungle training and acclimatisation, where they learn about the local culture and are taught kit packing, first aid, navigation, bivouac construction, river crossing, radio communication and abseiling. They are also briefed by scientists on site.

Recruitment all year

WORLD CHALLENGE EXPEDITIONS LTD

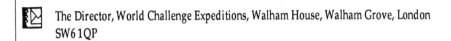

The Director, World Challenge Expeditions, Walham House, Walham Grove, London SW6 1QP

071-386 9828

Since 1988 there have been expeditions to Belize, Canada, Ecuador, Kenya, Malaysia, Morocco, Nepal, Pakistan, Thailand and Venezuela

Established in 1987, World Challenge runs adventure training expeditions for young people. Projects are designed to be fulfilling and enjoyable, giving a full chance for actual participation in leadership, a sense of environmental awareness and above all, a real challenge.

The detailed programme for each expedition will depend on the experience and wishes of the team. Trekking and exploration are combined with the study of local flora and fauna, and participants also have the opportunity to meet native and tribal peoples. Three expeditions are organised a year, each consisting of 2 leaders and up to 20 participants.

Ages 16-20. No experience or qualifications necessary. Applicants should have real enthusiasm, a desire to learn and travel, physical fitness and a willingness to face both physical and mental challenges. In all applicants motivation is considered more important than physical prowess.

4-5 weeks, beginning July

Expedition fee £2,100-£2,400 (1992) depending on destination. This covers flights, insurance, food, specialist equipment, emergency back-up and administration. 20% non-refundable deposit required to confirm the offer of a place.

Candidates' suitability and aptitude for an expedition is measured at an assessment weekend. 36 hour build-up training provided prior to departure.

Apply preferably before Christmas of the year prior to departure

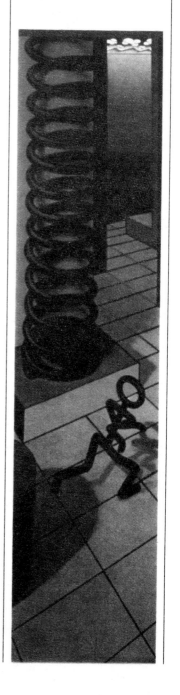

CONSERVATION / LAND USE

Conservation The Earth is 4,600 million years old; over the last 150 years we have come close to upsetting the ecological balance that has developed since the planet's creation. Earth's human inhabitants have raided the planet for fuels, used the land, sea and air as rubbish tips, and caused the extinction of over 500 species of animals. For those who believe and care about the future of planet Earth, and who would like to make some contribution, no matter how small, towards its health and management, a year out can present the ideal opportunity.

Work can be undertaken on a wide range of tasks: carrying out surveys to determine current population levels, habits or optimum environment of different species; building trails through forests and nature reserves; cleaning polluted rivers, ponds and lakes; stabilising sand dunes; or acting as an environmental interpreter in a nature centre. There are also plenty of opportunities to preserve the built environment, including the restoration of railways, canals and other aspects of our industrial heritage; conserving churches, castles and architectural monuments; renovating stately homes and gardens; rebuilding abandoned hamlets; preserving archaeological remains; and building drystone walls. Some projects include training on particular aspects of conservation work. All tasks involve work which could not otherwise be achieved without volunteer assistance. In addition to the recruiters detailed in this section, the organisations below undertake conservation work in Britain and recruit volunteers accordingly. Projects tend to be limited to 10 days at the most, and therefore will only be of interest as short-term alternatives for those having a year between. Most organisations have a local group network; volunteers wishing to join a group should contact headquarters for a list of addresses.

England & Wales
British Trust for Conservation Volunteers
Room WH, 36 St Mary's Street, Wallingford, Oxfordshire OX10 0EU
✆ Wallingford (0491) 39766

National Trust Acorn Camps Volunteer Unit, PO Box 12, Westbury, Wiltshire BA13 4NA
✆ Westbury (0373) 826826

Scotland
The Scottish Conservation Projects Trust
Balallan House, 24 Allan Park, Stirling FK8 2QG
✆ Stirling (0786) 79697

National Trust for Scotland Thistle Camps, 5 Charlotte Square, Edinburgh EH2 4DU
✆ 031-226 5922 ext 257

Northern Ireland
Conservation Volunteers Northern Ireland
137 University Street, Belfast BT7 1HP

National Trust Northern Ireland Region
Rowallane House, Saintfield, Ballynahinch, Co Down BT24 7LH ✆ (0238) 510721

Due to the nature of the work and the fact that much of it carries on outdoors, there is a wider variety of projects in Britain during the summer months, although opportunities do exist all through the year. Further details of organisations arranging short-term conservation projects and workcamps throughout Britain, Europe and even further afield are given in the Central Bureau's annual guidebook **Working Holidays**.

Kibbutzim/moshavim There are hundreds of kibbutzim and moshavim all over Israel, offering the opportunity to experience living and working in a small, independent community. The first kibbutz was established in 1909 by a group of individuals who wanted to form a community where there was no exploitation and no drive to accumulate individual wealth. The desire to establish a just society is the basic principle guiding kibbutz life, together with a commitment to undertake tasks important to the development of Israel and the Jewish people. There are now 250 kibbutzim throughout Israel providing a way of life for nearly 100,000, in which all means of production are owned by the community as a whole. The workforce consists of all members and any volunteers, who receive no wages but give their labour according to ability and in return receive in accordance with their needs.

Kibbutzim are democratic societies and all members have a voice in determining how the kibbutz is run. A general assembly meets weekly and committees discuss and resolve specialist problems. Kibbutzim welcome volunteers who are prepared to live and work within the community and abide by the kibbutz way of life. Volunteers share all communal facilities with kibbutz members, and should be capable of adapting to a totally new society.

The majority of work for volunteers is in the communal dining room, the laundry and possibly in children's houses. On most kibbutzim children live in houses apart from their parents, spending only part of the afternoons and evenings with them. This allows mothers to become active in the life of the kibbutz, and ensures an equality of education where the community as a whole is responsible for the care and education of the children.

Some of the work during summer months includes citrus, melon and soft fruit harvesting, and volunteers may also be involved in haymaking, gardening or working in the fish ponds, cow sheds or chicken houses. Part of the time is also likely to spent in non-specialist, light industrial work. Volunteers work approximately an 8 hour day, 6 day week with Saturdays free. Work

outdoors often starts at 05.00 and finishes at 14.00, the hottest part of the afternoons being free. Volunteers live together in wood cabins, 2-4 to a room, with food provided in the communal dining room.

Moshavim are collective settlements of from 10-100 individual smallholders. Each family works and develops its own area of land or farm while sharing the capital costs of equipment, marketing and necessary services. There are almost 1,000 moshavim where volunteers can live and work as a member of an Israeli family, mainly in the Jordan valley, the Arava and the western Negev. Most of the work is on the land, particularly in flower growing, market gardening and specialist fruit farming.

The main agencies in Britain recruiting volunteers to work on kibbutzim and moshavim are:

Kibbutz Representatives Volunteer Coordinator, 1a Accommodation Road, London NW11 8ED ✆ 081-458 9235

WST Charters Priory House, 6 Wrights Lane, London W8 6TA ✆ 071-938 4362

Gil Travel Ltd 65 Gloucester Place, London W1 3PF ✆ 071-935 1701

Project 67 Ltd 10 Hatton Garden, London EC1N 8AH ✆ 071-831 7626

Kibbutzim or moshavim volunteers should be aged 18-32, in good physical and mental health, and will need references, a medical certificate and a special entry visa. Volunteers should bear in mind that the work is often physically arduous, that conditions can be uncomfortable, and the hours long. The effect of living in relatively close confinement with a group of fellow volunteers is also something that should not be underestimated.

Placements on kibbutzim and moshavim can last from 5 weeks up to one year.

Agriculture/horticulture Placements abroad are available for young people considering an agricultural/horticultural career through the international exchange organisations listed in this section. There are also a limited number of placements available through GAP and Project Trust for young men to work as jackaroos on sheep/cattle stations. Farm placements are likely to involve fairly strenuous work; applicants should be physically fit, with a strong practical streak. A valid driving licence is often essential, and general maintenance skills will come in very useful.

There are also opportunities available in Britain for people, preferably with basic skills or qualifications in horticulture, to work on community garden projects involving horticultural therapy. Projects are based at hospitals, day centres, residential homes or urban farms and can range from small gardens to large commercial nurseries, reclaiming derelict land or creating new amenities. Volunteers may work alongside elderly or disadvantaged people, or people with physical handicaps, visual or hearing impairments, mental or psychiatric problems. They help to prepare and cultivate sites and train people in basic horticultural tasks, playing a key role in encouraging a team spirit amongst the project's gardeners. The rewards, in both shared experience and therapeutic benefit, can be many.

Jane worked for Land Use Volunteers, the volunteer service of the Society for Horticultural Therapy, which helps disabled and handicapped people enjoy and benefit from gardening, horticulture and agriculture:

I was very happy during my six months as a Land Use volunteer. Undoubtedly it provided me with very valuable experience, and it is certainly a time I shall never forget.

Australian Trust for Conservation Volunteers

Coral Cay Conservation Ltd

GAP Activity Projects (GAP) Ltd

H T Scotland

International Agricultural Exchange Association

International Farm Experience Programme

Involvement Volunteers

Land Use Volunteers

Project 67

The Project Trust

Student Conservation Association

AUSTRALIAN TRUST FOR CONSERVATION VOLUNTEERS

 The Executive Director, Australian Trust for Conservation Volunteers (ATCV), National Head Office, PO Box 423, Ballarat 3353, Victoria, Australia

 Ballarat (53) 331 483   Fax (53) 332 290

 Throughout Australia

 Set up in 1982, the Trust is a non-profit, non-political, community-based organisation which undertakes practical conservation projects involving volunteers in the management and care of the environment

 Echidna Package scheme enables overseas volunteers to work on ATCV projects. ATCV undertake approx 700 projects each year, including tree planting, constructing walking tracks and vermin proof fences, seed collection, protection of endangered animals and flora and fauna surveys.

 Ages 17+. Applicants should be fit and willing to work in a team. A sound knowledge of English necessary. Anti-tetanus immunisation essential. Volunteers are advised to enquire at the nearest Australian high commission, embassy or consulate regarding visa eligibility before requesting an application form from ATCV.

 6+ weeks

 Food, accommodation and travel whilst on project provided. Volunteers can be met on arrival at Melbourne, Sydney or Brisbane Airport, but must arrange their own travel to Australia, visitors' visa, medical and travel insurance. Discounts available for Echidna Package participants on both international flights and internal travel. Cost of package AU$500 for initial 6 weeks, AU$63 for each additional week.

 Apply at least 3 months in advance

CORAL CAY CONSERVATION LTD

The Director, Coral Cay Conservation Ltd, Sutton Business Centre, Restmor Way, Wallington, Surrey SM6 7AH

081-669 0011

Belize

A non-profitmaking organisation established in 1986 to provide the government of Belize with scientific expertise and resources for the management of the Belize Barrier Reef, which, second only in size to the Great Barrier Reef of Australia, is unique in the western hemisphere on account of its size, variety of reef types and quality of corals. With the recent boom in Belizean tourism and fishery industries, the reef is under serious threat of damage from uncontrolled exploitation of its resources.

Volunteers are invited to join scientific expeditions to help in surveying the reef area. Expeditions are made up of approx 30 volunteers divided into teams, each team having responsibility on a rota basis for a different aspect of expedition life: organising dive teams, preparation and maintenance of equipment, cooking and cleaning.

Ages 16+. Applicants should have a keen interest in conserving one of the world's greatest barrier reef systems. They should also be able to work as part of a team with other volunteers in a small island community. No scientific background is required, as training is given. Volunteers must be members of the British Sub-Aqua Club or have proof of diving ability through another recognised agency. Coray Cay can provide diving tuition through their branch of the British Sub-Aqua Club.

4-12 weeks

Approx 60 hour week: subject to weather conditions, at least two survey dives take place each day under the supervision of qualified marine scientists. Weekends are free for recreational diving, watersports or visits to rainforests, Mayan ruins or jaguar and howler monkey reserves. Cost from £1,600 for 4 weeks includes return flight, transit hotel accommodation, full board and basic accommodation on site, equipment hire and scientific training. Volunteers must obtain their own insurance, take adequate medical precautions and supply their own diving kit.

Volunteers are taught all they need to know about marine identification, underwater survey techniques, using and servicing equipment

Recruitment all year

GAP ACTIVITY PROJECTS (GAP) LTD

The Company Secretary, GAP Activity Projects, GAP House, 44 Queen's Road, Reading, Berkshire RG1 4BB

Australia, Falkland Islands, Israel

A charity founded in 1972 to give those with a year between leaving school and going on to further/higher education or vocational training the opportunity to work in another country

Arrange placements on sheep and wheat stations in Australia, on sheep farms in the Falkland Islands and on kibbutzim in Israel

Ages 18-19. UK nationals only. Males only for placements in Australia and the Falkland Islands. Applicants should be reliable, possess initiative and intelligence, and be prepared to work hard.

6 months.

Board and accommodation provided, and usually a small amount of pocket money. Volunteers must find their own travel and insurance costs, plus the placement fee of £150-£300, depending on country chosen.

Candidates attend a briefing session before departure

Apply early in September of last year at school; interviews held November-March

H T SCOTLAND

The Volunteer Coordinator, HT Scotland, 4 Drum Street, Gilmerton, Edinburgh EH17 8QG

031-658 1096

Scotland

A voluntary organisation founded in 1989 to provide advice, information and support to projects using horticulture in their work with people with disabilities

Volunteers are needed to work on horticultural projects with handicapped, disabled and disadvantaged people, at various places throughout Scotland.

Ages 18+. Applicants must be self-motivated with initiative and a desire to work with people from all walks of life, especially those with special needs. Qualifications, skills and/or basic experience in horticulture or gardening desirable. All nationalities considered. **B D PH**

6-12 months

Volunteers work approx 35 hours per week. Full board and lodging provided on or off site, plus £20 per week pocket money, insurance and initial travel expenses to project. One week's leave every four months, by arrangement with project management.

Some training given on-site, plus evaluation

Recruitment all year

INTERNATIONAL AGRICULTURAL EXCHANGE ASSOCIATION

The Coordinator, International Agricultural Exchange Association, YFC Centre, National Agricultural Centre, Kenilworth, Warwickshire CV8 2LG

Coventry (0203) 696578

Australia, Canada, Japan, New Zealand, United States. Two-country placements available; stopovers in Singapore, Thailand, Hawaii can be arranged en route.

Operates opportunities for young people involved with agriculture, horticulture or home management to acquire practical work experience in the rural sector and to strengthen and improve their knowledge and understanding of the way of life in other countries.

Participants are given the opportunity to study practical methods on approved training farms, and work as trainees, gaining further experience in their chosen field

Ages 18-30. UK or Irish passport-holders only. Applicants should have a real desire for a farming and cultural experience abroad. They must be single, have good practical experience in the category of work they have chosen and hold a valid driver's licence.

6-14 months, depending on placement

Cost from £1,370, depending on country chosen. £200 deposit payable. Costs cover airfare, work permit, administration fee, insurance, supervision, placement, information and orientation. Trainees live as members of host family and receive £50-£60 per week. Supervisors visit trainees and host families at least once during programme. All programmes include at least 3 weeks unpaid holiday.

All trainees attend an information meeting prior to departure, where they meet past trainees and support staff. Compulsory orientation seminars are conducted in the host country.

Apply at least 4 months in advance

INTERNATIONAL FARM EXPERIENCE PROGRAMME

The Organiser, International Farm Experience Programme, YFC Centre, National Agricultural Centre, Kenilworth, Warwickshire, CV8 2LG

Coventry (0203) 696584

Austria, China, Denmark, Finland, France, Germany, Hungary, Israel, Netherlands, Norway, Poland, Sweden, Switzerland, United States

Provides assistance to young farmers and horticulturalists by finding them places in farms/nurseries abroad. This enables them to broaden their knowledge of the industry, learn new skills and techniques, make new friends and expand their personal horizons.

Opportunities for practical agricultural and horticultural work on a variety of farms and nurseries. Participants usually live and work with a farmer's family, and work is matched as far as possible with participants' requirements. Au pair positions also available for young women in some countries.

Ages 18-26. Applicants must have at least 2 years practical experience, 1 year of which may be at an agricultural college, and intend to make a career in agriculture/horticulture. Valid driving licence essential.

Usually 3-12 months

Participants generally work an 8-10 hour day, 6 day week, with every other weekend free, and receive £30 per week plus board and lodging. They pay their own fares and insurance. Registration fee £70.

Also offer 3-4 month practical training courses in all EC countries, which can be preceded by 5 week French or German course in France. Some of the programmes in the United States include a university course, where participants can study an aspect of the industry in detail.

Apply at least 4 months in advance

INVOLVEMENT VOLUNTEERS

 The Director, Involvement Volunteers, PO Box 218, Port Melbourne, Victoria 3207, Australia

 Melbourne (3) 646 5504

 Australia, Fiji, India, Thailand, United States (California, Hawaii)

 Aims to assist people travelling overseas to participate as volunteers in community-based, non-profitmaking organisations throughout Australia and a growing number of countries en route

 Individual or team placements include conservation projects: in urban or rural areas; on farms planting trees; marine archaeology; zoology research; bird observatory operations; researching, restoring or maintaining historic sites or gardens; developing National Parks or recreation areas; assisting native villages or agricultural education programmes related to sustainable agricultural development.

 Ages 17+. Relevant experience welcome but only necessary for certain projects. Understanding of spoken English essential.

 4+ weeks; no limit to the number of placements

 Cost AU$300. Involvement Volunteers provides advice on placements, itinerary planning, meeting on arrival; and in Australia initial accommodation, introductions to banking and a communications base. Discounted internal travel available. Board and accommodation vary according to placement, and cannot always be provided free of charge. Volunteers arrange their own visitor visa, international travel and insurance.

 Apply 3 months in advance if possible, to get the best placements

LAND USE VOLUNTEERS

The Volunteer Coordinator, Land Use Volunteers, Horticultural Therapy, Goulds Ground, Vallis Way, Frome, Somerset BA11 3DW

Frome (0373) 464782

England and Wales

The Society for Horticultural Therapy is a non-profitmaking company founded in 1978 to help disabled and handicapped people enjoy and benefit from gardening, horticulture and agriculture. Land Use Volunteers, its volunteer service, began in 1981 and is one of a wide range of practical services offered to disabled people and those who work with them.

Volunteers are needed to work with handicapped, disabled and disadvantaged people, living and working on rehabilitation projects on the basis of a common interest in plants and animals to enable land use activities work more effectively. Past projects have included developing a small hospital market garden whilst working with psychiatric patients and care staff; working with adult mentally handicapped residents at a home farm, breeding rare domestic animals and organic growing; training clients and other care staff in simple horticultural tasks; and working with ex-drug addicts and offenders in planting and gardening. Also work with the physically handicapped, the hearing impaired, the blind, the elderly and disturbed young people.

Ages 18+. Applicants must be self-confident, adaptable, able to fit into a small community with a desire to transmit their qualifications, skills and/or basic experience in agriculture, horticulture, forestry or any related discipline. All nationalities considered. Knowledge of English required. B D PH

6-12 months

Full board and lodging provided on or off site, plus £20 pocket money per week and initial travel expenses to project. One week vacation every four weeks, by arrangement with project management.

Recruitment all year

PROJECT 67

 The Managing Director, Project 67, 10 Hatton Garden, London EC1N 8AH

 071-831 7626

 Israel

 As the official representatives in the UK of the Ha'Artzi Kibbutz Movement, Project 67 has organised working holidays on kibbutzim and moshavim in Israel for the past 20 years

 A kibbutz is a communal society in which the means of production are owned by the community as a whole. Volunteers work alongside permanent residents and other volunteers; work can include farmwork, market gardening and light industry. A moshav is a collective of individual smallholders where each family develops its own land whilst sharing capital costs. Volunteers live and work as part of a family; work can include flower, vegetable or fruit growing, or chicken and dairy farming.

 Ages 18-32 (kibbutzim); 21-35 (moshavim). Applicants must be physically and mentally fit. No formal skills, qualifications or experience necessary.

 5 weeks-12 months

 Cost from £285 (kibbutzim) or from £265 (moshavim) covers return flight, registration and support from Tel Aviv office. Volunteers work an 8 hour day, 5 day week, or a 6½ hour day, 6 day week and receive full board, lodging and an allowance.

 Briefing held in London by the Kibbutz Movement to advise on conditions and give opportunity to meet fellow volunteers. No briefing necessary for moshavim.

 Apply as early as possible; places are limited. Last-minute applications are sometimes accepted.

THE PROJECT TRUST

 The Director, Project Trust, Breacachadh Castle, Isle of Coll, Argyll PA78 6TB

 Coll (087 93) 444

 Australia

 Founded in 1968, Project Trust is a non-sectarian educational trust sending British school leavers overseas for a year between school and further/higher education or commerce/industry. Its aims are to enable a new generation to experience life and work overseas, gaining some understanding of life outside Europe, particularly in the Third World, and to place volunteers in a way which is of real benefit to the community.

 Projects are specifically chosen to ensure that volunteers are not taking work from local people. As well as teaching and community work placements worldwide there are also opportunities to work as jackaroos at sheep or cattle stations in Australia. Recruits 200 volunteers annually.

 Males only for these positions. Applicants must be at least 17.3 years, maximum 19 years at time of going overseas. They should have initiative, commonsense, flexibility and sensitivity and be physically fit and healthy to cope with the climate and conditions. Open to UK passport-holders in full-time education, taking 3 A levels (or equivalent).

 One year, starting August/September

 Volunteers live in the same type of accommodation as a local worker, with food usually provided. Insurance, travel and £25 per month pocket money paid. Leave is at the discretion of the host. Cost £2,500 of which volunteers must earn at least £150 by themselves and raise the rest through sponsorship.

 Initial interviews held June-January at a location close to the applicant's home; between September and April successful candidates attend a four day selection course on the Isle of Coll, costing £90 plus travel, and deductible from sponsorship money. The island's few inhabitants play a major rôle in the selection and training of volunteers and this, plus the history of Coll give volunteers an invaluable insight into the conditions to be met overseas. Compulsory training course held in July; candidates learn the rudiments of teaching and are briefed on their project. Two day debriefing course on return.

Applications open 14 months before proposed date of departure

STUDENT CONSERVATION ASSOCIATION

Resource Assistant Program, Student Conservation Association Inc, PO Box 550, Charlestown, New Hampshire 03603, United States

(603) 826-4301   Fax (603) 826 7755

Throughout the United States, including Hawaii, Alaska and the US Virgin Islands

Founded in 1957, the Student Conservation Association is a national non-profitmaking organisation committed to conservation, resource management and volunteer service

The SCA works with state, federal and private organisations to place volunteers in over 250 national parks, forests, wildlife refuges and similar areas each year. Duties vary with location, but may include trail patrol, wildlife management, visitor contact, natural science interpretation, forestry, archaeological surveys or recreation management.

Ages 18+. Applicants should have an interest in conservation or resource management. Some positions may require experience in public speaking, hiking or other outdoor activities, or in a particular academic field.

12+ weeks

Volunteers receive $45-$90 per week to cover food expenses, and a uniform allowance if required. Accommodation is provided in an apartment, trailer or ranger station. SCA offer information and assistance with visas, and partial travel reimbursement within the USA. Application fee $15.

Training, guidance and supervision provided by professional staff

SCA supply application forms and a current listing of positions available. Apply 2 months in advance.

TEACHING/
INSTRUCTING

TEACHING/INSTRUCTING

English has become the international language of air traffic, popular media communication, business, science and technology, and as a result the teaching of English as a foreign language provides an interesting opportunity to undertake a challenging period of work in either Britain or abroad.

However a TEFL (Teaching of English as a Foreign Language) or TESOL (Teaching of English to Speakers of Other Languages) certificate is required for most placements, and anyone contemplating TEFL work even on a short-term basis should think carefully about the amount of work involved. Many TEFL teachers are expected to work long hours as well as taking time to prepare lessons and supervise recreational and leisure activities. Most of the openings for work in private language schools are for those with a recognised TEFL qualification and/or experience. Many language schools in Britain offer introductory TEFL training and their own qualifications. However the initial qualifications that are the most widely recognised on an international level are the Royal Society of Arts/University of Cambridge Local Examinations Syndicate (RSA/UCLES) and Trinity College London TESOL certificates.

Applicants for the RSA/UCLES certificate follow a 4/5 weeks full-time approved course. Part-time programmes are offered at some centres and there a number of approved centres overseas. Participants should have a good standard of education, usually two A levels or equivalent, and should ensure they have no other commitments for the duration of the course. The Certificate is awarded on the successful completion of the course which assesses written and practical work. Further details of the RSA Certificate courses, syllabus and assessment are available from UCLES, Syndicate Buildings, 1 Hills Road, Cambridge CB1 2EU.

Both native and non-native speakers of English are eligible for the Trinity College TESOL Certificate. Applicants follow an approved training course, usually available on a part-time basis and assessment is on theoretical and practical knowledge. Some courses combine a short intensive study with distance learning. Further information on the courses and assessment is available from Trinity College London, 16 Park Crescent, London W1N 4AH ℡ 071-323 2328.

Those with two or more years experience of teaching EFL can apply for a diploma course, also available through RSA/UCLES and Trinity College. Most of the courses are part-time, usually two evenings study per week over one academic year.

As well as the opportunities covered in this section, many TEFL posts are advertised in the national press, such as the Educational Appointments section of the *Guardian* (every Tuesday) or the specialist education press such as the *Times Educational Supplement* (every Friday). Applicants should find out as much as possible about the school and make sure they have a proper contract and work permit (where necessary) before accepting a position. Schools that are approved or recognised by a national inspecting body are likely to operate to good standards. As a rule, you should not be expected to teach much more than 25 hours per week, with a maximum of 20 students per class, but on top of this you will need to prepare classes and may also be required for supervisory duties.

Teaching English Abroad is a guide to short and long-term TEFL opportunities. Available from Vacation Work, 9 Park End Street, Oxford OX1 1HJ ℡Oxford (0865) 241978, price £7.95.

International House, 106 Piccadilly, London W1V 9FL ℂ 071-491 2598 can provide details of TEFL courses including the RSA Diploma TEFLA course and job opportunities through its own network of schools.

ARELS-FELCO (Association of Recognised English Language Schools/Federation of English Language Colleges), 2 Pontypool Place, Valentine Place, London SE1 8QF operates a monitoring sytem for TEFL schools and courses in conjunction with the British Council. A list of member schools is available, to which direct applications can be made by qualified TEFL teachers.

Opportunities for school leavers to undertake TEFL teaching are limited, and usually consist of acting as helpers to English language teachers or teaching on a voluntary basis in the Third World. Work is also available in Britain, and occasionally abroad, for post-A level students to act as student teachers or assistant matrons in independent schools. As well as teaching, work usually involves domestic and supervisory duties. Those interested may either approach schools direct, or apply through the relevant organisations listed in this section.

The Central Bureau's annual guide **Working Holidays** has further details on short-term TEFL opportunities, including opportunities on English language summer camps in a number of European countries. For those with some teaching or instructing skills and qualifications or relevant experience **Working Holidays** also offers a variety of other opportunities, including instructing on activity holidays and general and sports coaching duiring the summer holidays.

Keran, Tania and Daniel worked as junior language Assistants in France and Spain during their year between. Under this scheme, run by the Central Bureau for Educational Visits & Exchanges, participants work under the supervision of the English teaching staff, improving the pupils' command of spoken English and introducing them to British life, customs and institutions. Keran relished the challenge of teaching in a French state secondary school:

I have undoubtedly experienced the best six months of my life, learning how to live independently. My French is now fluent, though not always accurate. I have integrated very well into the French way of life. Teaching a class of thirty rowdy children who are almost the same age as you is the greatest challenge, but a very enjoyable and satisfying one. I learnt exactly what it was like to be standing in front of the blackboard. This six months helped me to decide that I want to be a teacher. I have learned a great deal about the French education system from all levels (teachers, children, surveillants). This is a very productive and pleasurable way of spending six months before going into higher education.

Tania, who also worked in France, felt that the time spent as an *assistant à temps partiel* gave her increased confidence and forced her to use her dormant creative imagination:

I have learned a lot about how to deal with schoolchildren and about how to teach. I have learned a lot about life in France through mixing with all sorts of different people. I've made some brilliant friends amongst other Assistants here. My French has improved no end (though I fear it is now irreversibly colloquial!). I have gained a lot of confidence by coming to a foreign country knowing no one and discovering such a lot, meeting so many people and having such a good time. I have exercised my imagination as I haven't done since I was a child, thinking up entertaining and useful lessons. I also have enjoyed having time to relax - time I never give myself at home.

Daniel spent two terms in an independent Spanish secondary boarding school. He assisted in the classroom and took small groups of pupils in conversation practice:

The Assistant scheme is a wonderful opportunity to immerse yourself completely in a foreign culture and language. My Spanish improved by the minute and the Spanish people were extremely warm, helpful and hospitable.

French Encounters is an independent enterprise running vacation study courses for children in France. It finds that those having a year between that they employ as *animateurs* and *animatrices* to help run the courses considerably increase in awareness and maturity during their time spent there. In addition, foreign language competence is greatly enhanced.

However, if you are going to teach in your year between you should be aware that the majority of your students are likely to be young teenagers, and you will need patience, energy and a real liking of working with children if you are to make a success of the task in hand. Your creative resources may be tested to the limit in order to put over imaginatively the language concepts you are attempting to teach. Having just completed over a dozen years of continuous education yourself you will need to have the ability and understanding to motivate others who may be only reluctantly committed to additional learning.

That apart, the rewards to be gained from a period of teaching are not to be underestimated. The work may be challenging and exhausting but it can also be deeply satisfying, using your creative skills to pass on knowledge and to awaken interest in even the most seemingly uninterested and unmotivated student.

Association à l'Initiation et Formation en

Anglais (AIFA)

French Encounters

Gabbitas, Truman & Thring

GAP Activity Projects (GAP) Ltd

Involvement Volunteers

Japan Exchange & Teaching (JET)

Programme

Junior Language Assistants

Language Assistants

The Project Trust

Q E D

Schools' Partnership Worldwide

ASSOCIATION A L'INITIATION ET FORMATION EN ANGLAIS (AIFA)

Responsable des Intervenants, Association à l'Initiation et Formation en Anglais (AIFA), c/o Les Courauds, 4460 Maisdon sur Sèvre, France

40 06 66 10

The Montaigu area of Vendée

An organisation set up by the Young Chamber of Commerce of North Vendée, aimed at introducing the English language to children at primary school

Three posts are available to teach English in primary schools

Ages 18-21. UK nationals only. Applicants must have A level French (or equivalent) with good oral skills, experience of living or travelling abroad and of working with young children. A love of children and a desire to teach are also essential, as are good organisational skills, independence, initiative and an interest in the French way of life.

9 months, beginning October

Participants work 22 hours per week and receive a salary of FF1,500 per month. Board and lodging is provided with local families. Participants pay their own travel and insurance costs.

Training is given during the first week, and participants are expected to write a report during their placement

Apply as early as possible

FRENCH ENCOUNTERS

Soula Callow, Managing Director, French Encounters, 63 Fordhouse Road, Bromsgrove, Worcestershire B60 2LU

Bromsgrove (0527) 73645

Normandy

A small, independent enterprise running vacation study courses for 10-13 year old children, based in two *châteaux* in Normandy.

Animateurs/trices are required to help run the courses. Work involves accompanying coaches and giving commentaries on places to be visited; supervising children on visits and picnics; organising indoor and outdoor activities and evening entertainment; encouraging children to speak French and eat French food; and generally making their stay a pleasant and rewarding one. Recruits 4-8 *animateurs/trices* annually.

Ages 18-22. UK nationals only. Applicants should have enthusiasm, good organisational skills, the ability to work as part of a team, self discipline and a sense of humour. Experience of working with 10-13 year old children, plus A level French with good oral skills essential.

4 months, beginning February

Animateurs/trices work approx 35 hours per week, but as they are resident in the *châteaux* they are on call 24 hours a day. Full board and lodging is provided, plus £35 per week pocket money. All transport costs and insurance are provided.

Compulsory training course and debriefing provided before and after period of work

Apply before 25 September. Interviews are held in the first week of October.

GABBITAS, TRUMAN & THRING

 Gabbitas, Truman & Thring, Broughton House, 6-8 Sackville Street, London W1X 2BR

071-734 0161 or 071-439 2071

Throughout the UK

A non-profitmaking company dedicated to giving expert advice and guidance to parents and students. Advice covers the choice of independent schools, colleges and courses; planning and preparing for higher education; career guidance and options for a year out.

Recruits teaching and non-teaching staff for independent schools and colleges. Approx 30 positions are available each year.

Ages 17/18+. No experience or qualifications necessary, but school leavers should have A levels or equivalent and be going on to university. A good school record and plenty of outside interests are desirable. Overseas applicants must have the appropriate visa/work permit and be available for interview.

3-9 months

Terms and conditions of work vary according to placement. Full board accommodation usually provided within the school, in addition to salary.

Apply by June/July to begin the following academic year

GAP ACTIVITY PROJECTS (GAP) LTD

The Company Secretary, GAP Activity Projects, GAP House, 44 Queen's Road, Reading, Berkshire RG1 4BB

Africa: Namibia, South Africa
Asia: China, India, Indonesia, Malaysia, Nepal, Pakistan
Europe: Bulgaria, Czechoslovakia, Hungary, Poland, USSR
Latin America: Chile, Ecuador, Falkland Islands
North America: Canada, United States
Pacific: Australia

A charity founded in 1972 to give those with a year between leaving school and going on to further/higher education or vocational training the opportunity to work in another country.

Attachments are available in schools, which may involve teaching English, or in English-speaking countries, acting as teachers' assistants and coaching in games, music or drama

Ages 18-19. UK nationals only. Applicants should be reliable, possess initiative and intelligence, and be prepared to work hard. Those working on Latin American and Russian projects must be able to speak the relevant language.

Most placements are for 6 months; some for 9-12 months

Board and accommodation provided, and usually a small amount of pocket money. Volunteers must find their own travel and insurance costs, plus the placement fee of £150-£300, depending on country chosen. For many teaching placements applicants must attend a 1 week TEFL course.

Candidates attend a briefing session before departure

Apply early in September of last year at school. Interviews held November-March.

INVOLVEMENT VOLUNTEERS

 The Director, Involvement Volunteers, PO Box 218, Port Melbourne, Victoria 3207, Australia

 Melbourne (3) 646 5504

 Australia, Fiji, India, Thailand, United States (California, Hawaii)

 Aims to assist people travelling overseas to participate as volunteers in community-based, non-profitmaking organisations throughout Australia and a growing number of countries en route.

 Placements are available to suit local needs which vary from teaching children with learning difficulties to assisting local teachers of English as a second language; occupational therapy for the rehabilitation of mentally handicapped children; recreation for elderly people; social welfare related training for volunteer organisations; and health care instruction in villages.

 Ages 17+, depending on requirement of placement. Relevant experience welcome, but not always necessary for certain projects. Understanding of spoken English essential.

 6-8+ weeks

 Cost AU$300. Involvement Volunteers provides advice, placements and arrangements, itinerary planning, meeting on arrival; and in Australia initial accommodation, introductions to banking and a communications base. Discounted internal travel available. Board and accommodation vary according to placement, and cannot always be provided free of charge. Volunteers arrange their own visitor visa, international travel and insurance;

 Apply at least 3 months in advance; more planning time is recommended if possible

JAPAN EXCHANGE AND TEACHING (JET) PROGRAMME

JET Assistant, JET Programme Desk, Council for International Educational Exchange, 33 Seymour Place, London W1H 8AT

071-224 8896

Japan

Seeks to promote mutual understanding between Japan and other countries, and fosters international perspectives by promoting international exchange and intensifying foreign language education in Japan. Conducted under the co-sponsorship of the Japanese Ministries of Foreign Affairs, Education and Home Affairs and local governments.

Vacancies for English teaching assistants, carrying out coaching in English language and pronunciation, preparing teaching materials and participating in extra-curricular activities, under the guidance of Japanese academic staff. Placements are in lower and upper secondary schools.

Ages 21-35. Applicants must be mentally and physically fit, with an interest in Japan and the ability to adapt themselves to living and working conditions significantly different to those experienced at home. They should be interested in education and teaching in general, and in the teaching of the English language in particular. Applicants must be British nationals holding a Bachelor's degree. They must have excellent English pronunciation, rhythm, intonation and voice projection, good English writing skills and grammar usage. Teaching experience or training an advantage. Knowledge of Japanese not essential, but candidates are expected to devote some effort to learning the language before leaving for Japan and while they are there.

12 months, beginning late July

Participants work on average 40 hours per week. Salary Y3,600,000 per annum, tax free; paid holiday on similar terms to Japanese colleagues. Return air ticket provided, and assistance given with finding accommodation.

Participants receive written information on the programme and on basic Japanese before departure. Further orientation provided on arrival in Tokyo.

Apply by mid December; interviews take place February/March. Application forms available from October.

JUNIOR LANGUAGE ASSISTANTS

 Assistants Department, Central Bureau for Educational Visits & Exchanges, Seymour Mews House, Seymour Mews, London W1H 9PE

 071-486 5101

 France, Germany, Spain

 The Central Bureau for Educational Visits and Exchanges was set up in 1948 by the British government to act as the national office for the provision of information and advice on all forms of educational visits and exchanges.

 Vacancies for junior language Assistants to work in secondary schools under the supervision of the English teaching staff. Junior language Assistants may also take small groups of pupils to improve their command of spoken English and give them an insight into British life, customs and institutions, and are expected to participate fully in the life of the school. The number of posts is limited and competition is very strong. Only a very small number of posts are available in Germany. Applicants should be prepared to attend interview in London at their own expense.

 Ages 18-20. Applicants must have an A level (or equivalent) in the language of the country in which they wish to work.

 6 months, January-June

 12-15 hours teaching per week, including some recreational activities. Board, lodging and monthly allowance provided. Travel costs not provided. Registration fee £5.

 Short introductory briefing session held either at the Central Bureau or in country of appointment before taking up duty

 Application deadlines: France, by first week in June; Germany, by 31 March; Spain, by mid September.

LANGUAGE ASSISTANTS

 Assistants Department, Central Bureau for Educational Visits & Exchanges, Seymour Mews House, Seymour Mews, London W1H 9PE

 071-486 5101

 Africa: Senegal   Europe: Austria, Belgium, Czechoslovakia, Denmark, France, Germany, Hungary, Italy, Liechtenstein, Netherlands, Spain, Sweden, Switzerland, USSR
Latin America: Argentina, Chile, Colombia, Costa Rica, Ecuador, Mexico, Paraguay, Peru, Uruguay, Venezuala   North America: Canada (Quebec)

 The Central Bureau for Educational Visits & Exchanges was set up in 1948 by the British government to act as the national office for the provision of information and advice on all forms of educational visits and exchanges.

 English language Assistants are assigned to schools or colleges abroad, where their rôle is to help the teachers of English in every way they can. Although the nature and range of activities involved will vary from post to post the main task of an Assistant is to improve pupils' English language skills, particularly listening and speaking, and to present aspects of the anglophone culture they represent. Work is usually carried out in small groups and almost always in close cooperation with the teacher.

 Ages 20-30. Native speakers of English only. Most applicants will have completed at least 2 years of a degree or diploma course, usually in the language of the country for which they are applying. Minimum relevant language requirement is an A level (or equivalent) pass. For some countries, graduates with teaching experience preferred. Where the number of applications exceeds the number of posts available, preference is given to undergraduates for whom a year abroad is a course requirement.

 Minimum 1 academic year

 Terms and conditions of service vary according to the country. Assistants work between 12 and 20 hours per week and receive a monthly allowance. They must be prepared to find their own accommodation although advice/assistance is usually offered. In most cases travel costs are not provided. Registration fee £10.

 Introductory courses, briefings or in-service training held, depending on the country

 Completed application forms and all requisite documents should reach the Central Bureau by the beginning of December prior to the year in which the opportunity is sought.

THE PROJECT TRUST

 The Director, Project Trust, Breacachadh Castle, Isle of Coll, Argyll PA78 6TB

 Coll (087 93) 444

 Africa: Botswana, Egypt, Namibia, South Africa, Zimbabwe.
Asia: China, Hong Kong, Indonesia, Japan, Pakistan, Thailand.
Latin America: Brazil, Honduras.
Australia, Jamaica, Jordan.

 Founded in 1968, Project Trust is a non-sectarian educational trust sending British school leavers overseas for a year between school and further/higher education or commerce/industry. Its aims are to enable a new generation to experience life and work overseas, gaining some understanding of life outside Europe, particularly in the Third World, and to place volunteers in a way which is of real benefit to the community.

 Projects are specifically chosen to ensure that volunteers are not taking work from local people. Opportunities include teaching English, arts and sciences, acting as teachers aides or helping at Outward Bound schools. Recruits 200 volunteers annually.

 Applicants must be at least 17.3 years, maximum 19 years at time of going overseas. They should have initiative, commonsense, flexibility and sensitivity and be physically fit and healthy to cope with the climate and conditions. Open to UK passport-holders in full-time education, taking 3 A levels (or equivalent).

 One year, starting August/September

 Volunteers live in the same type of accommodation as a local worker, with food usually provided. Insurance, travel and £25 per month pocket money paid. Leave is at the discretion of the host country. Cost £2,500 of which volunteers must earn at least £150 by themselves and raise the rest through sponsorship.

 Initial interviews held June-January at a location close to the applicant's home; between September and April successful candidates attend a four day selection course on the Isle of Coll, costing £90 plus travel, and deductible from sponsorship money. The island's few inhabitants play a major rôle in the selection and training of volunteers and this, plus the history of Coll give volunteers an invaluable insight into the conditions to be met overseas. Compulsory training course held in July; candidates learn the rudiments of teaching and are briefed on their project. Two day debriefing course on return.

 Applications open 14 months before proposed date of departure

Q E D

The Director, Q E D Educational Consultants, 2 High Street, Chesham, Buckinghamshire HP5 1EP

Chesham (0494) 773393

Throughout the UK

An educational consultancy offering a specialised recruitment service for teachers and students.

Places 2-3 school leavers each year, usually in independent preparatory schools for 8-13 year olds, where they work as games assistants or general teaching assistants

Ages 18-21. Applicants should have good A level (or equivalent) results and a range of extra curricular activities.

1-3 terms

Pay and conditions of work vary according to the placement, but in general staff are provided with full board accommodation in addition to salary

Recruitment all year

SCHOOLS' PARTNERSHIP WORLDWIDE

 The Director, Schools' Partnership Worldwide, 1 Catton Street, London WC1R 4AB

Schools' Partnership Worldwide, Westminster School, 17 Dean's Yard, London SW1P 3PB

 071-831 1603

 Nepal, Zimbabwe

 An educational charity, partly funded by the Overseas Development Administration, committed to promoting closer contact between the UK educational services and those in the developing world. One of its functions is to provide opportunities for member schools to focus guaranteed funding on overseas schools and projects, in return for which selected school leavers are able to work in those same countries in the year between school and further education. Some 160 positions are offered each year.

 Overseas secondment to English-medium government secondary schools in the Harare area of Zimbabwe and throughout Nepal. Participants undertake a full adult timetable, teaching English, Maths and other useful subjects up to GCSE level standard in understaffed and under-resourced schools. Secondments are in pairs, ideally of two close friends of the same sex.

 Ages 18-21. UK nationals only. Applicants should be expecting to gain high A level grades and have a real commitment to teaching; relevant experience an advantage. Flexibility and an openness to other cultures are essential, as is the resourcefulness to cope with living in spartan conditions. D PH accepted where practicable

 7-11 months, beginning September/October or January

 Priority is given to those applying from member schools; those from non-member schools have to be strongly recommended by their school and will need to raise £600 sponsorship in lieu of the school's subscription. Advice is given on fundraising. Participants pay their own airfare (£500-£600) and £10 per month insurance. Basic accommodation is provided, usually on a self-catering basis. In Zimbabwe student teachers are paid according to local rates; those in Nepal have to provide their own pocket money.

 Compulsory teacher training and induction courses, including basic instruction in Nepali where relevant, are held in London prior to departure; cost approx £60.

 Early application advised

COMMUNITY & SOCIAL SERVICE

There are many opportunities for those taking a year between to embark upon a period of community service. This can be a particularly valuable experience for everyone, but especially for those contemplating a career in health care or social work.

The work is classed as voluntary, but this does not necessarily imply that you work for nothing. Most volunteer placements provide board and lodging, plus a certain amount of pocket money, or if the placement is in the Third World, a wage according to local rates of pay. Applicants should however be aware that any type of community work involves commitment. The ideas and attitudes of voluntary service which used to be expressed as *helping those less fortunate than ourselves* or as *giving benefit to people in need* are inappropriate and patronising in society today.

School leavers should bear in mind that opportunities for unskilled volunteers to work in the Third World are now extremely limited. As well as the fact that these countries may themselves already have large numbers of unskilled, unemployed young people, it is also the case that most voluntary agencies need to recruit people with specialist skills and/or experience. However, there are a number of volunteer-sending agencies who can place school leavers on a year out. You could also try to find a placement through contacts with friends abroad, or by using links set up by your school or church.

Many agencies organising volunteer placements in the Third World will require you to raise money towards the cost of participation, or at least pay your own travel and living costs. You may wonder why, if you are going to be performing a voluntary service, you are also expected to pay your way. There are a number of reasons for this,

the overriding one being to reduce to a minimum any costs involved on the part of the agency who have to finance the project in terms of equipment, materials and administration. The host community itself is likely to be too poor to be expected to contribute; Britain in comparison is rich and a little effort on your part is all that is required to finance your trip. There is also a philosophy that those fortunate enough to have the opportunities of higher education or travel abroad have benefited from the resources available in their society, resources which are extremely limited in the Third World. Viewed from this angle a voluntary project can be seen as an educational and cultural experience, as well as a period of service to the community.

However you don't have to travel abroad to find out about other cultures. Britain's population, for example, is made up of many cultures and many faiths, and there are plenty of opportunities to work with them. You could also do a period of community service in another European country or in North America. If you have set your sights on working in the Third World you may not have realised that Western countries are also in need of volunteers. Working to overcome problems caused by disability, poverty, bad housing, illiteracy, unemployment and discrimination against an immigrant population in your own country is a very worthwhile challenge, and you won't need to raise a large sum of money in order to participate.

Community Service Volunteers is one of the largest organisations placing volunteers in Britain. Everyone aged 16 to 35 who can spend 4-12 months working full-time, away from home with people who need their help can be a Community Service Volunteer. Nearly 80% of the 2,500 CSVs placed each year are aged 17 to 22. They come from all walks of life: no one is ever turned away. For many the experience of community work marks a milestone in their life. Zoe Crosskey lost her place at university because of disappointing A levels:

I panicked. I nearly rushed into the first place I was offered, but my parents persuaded me to take a year off. They wanted me to see another aspect of life and think about what I really wanted to do.

After an interview at one of CSV's local offices, Zoe was given a six month position at a day centre in London helping adults with disabilities to develop new skills. She helped teach assertiveness training, supervised pottery workshops or spent time taking someone out to the shops. Zoe admitted it could be tough, but she'd recommend it to anyone, and thinks that doing badly in A levels might have been the best thing that could have happened. Partly because of her volunteer work, Zoe was offered a place at Southampton to study social administration.

Richard Washington, from Brenchley in Kent, worked on two CSV placements during a year between school and reading history at Oxford. Richard's first project was in Birmingham, helping a man with muscular dystrophy live in his own home, rather than in a residential institution. His second CSV placement took him to London, where he worked at a day centre for people with learning difficulties.

The placements were an eye-opener for him, as was his close contact with people with disabilities:

The concept that people who have disabilities are perfectly useless in society is so wrong; there is so much they have to give. CSV's changed my whole outlook. I feel I've matured mentally. Although it's difficult to pin down how, I feel different from the way I did 6 or 7 months ago. I would recommend it very strongly.

Of course, while volunteers gain a lot from their time as a CSV, the people they help benefit too. Angie Dobson has cerebral palsy. She is able to live in her own home and not in a residential institution through the support of CSV volunteers:

If it wasn't for the CSVs, I wouldn't be able to live in this flat and live my own life. I need a lot of help every day to do the things I want to do. Having CSVs means I can be my own person and be independent - which means a lot to me.

Being a CSV is tough, hard work, but it is also fun. CSVs take on serious responsibility, face new challenges and develop confidence and independence. Young people taking a year between benefit from their time as a CSV - and the community does too.

Many aspects of community and social service can be physically and emotionally draining, and you should read carefully all the literature provided on the project and consider your own strengths and weaknesses before formally applying. If you have any doubts or questions, discuss them thoroughly with the people running the project. The ability to take initiatives within the framework of the project team, to cope with crises, to exert discipline without being authoritarian, and to maintain a sense of humour and perspective, is usually essential. You may not be aware of possessing all these capabilities, but the training and experience provided by a period of community service may well bring them to the fore. This can only stand you in good stead and prepare you for the challenges you may face in your future career.

Sarah was a volunteer working in the Israeli-occupied Gaza Strip for the Universities Educational Fund for Paletinian Refugees (UNIPAL):

For me it was the first time I had got outside the European/American eyeview to see a different kind of society, a different way of thought and action ... this was made possible by the incredible welcome I was given by the Palestinians themselves. Throughout my stay I felt greatly my privilege at being welcomed by them as a sister.

Despite increasing demand from overseas for their volunteers, Project Trust, a non-sectarian educational trust sending British school leavers overseas in their year between, keeps their numbers low so that every volunteer is known personally to the Trust and is looked upon as an individual. Project Trust wants each volunteer to obtain maximum benefit from his/her time overseas, and they believe this is best achieved by getting the volunteers to identify with, and learn as much as they can, from the host community. The community involvement can take many forms: Mary and Kate worked as teachers at a secondary school in the midst of a community made up of mud hut villages and farms in Zimbabwe; there were up to 40 pupils to a class and the age range was wide. Ian and Charles worked at Ikhwezi Lokusa, a community home for physically handicapped children in the Transkei. Generally the children were crippled from diseases connected with malnutrition and poor living conditions, but the atmosphere of the home was one of hope. In Jordan, Simon and Tom lived and worked at a home for the mentally handicapped on the outskirts of Amman, stimulating the children's interests by teaching them all forms of art. For many the year between is their first long-term job experience, and can reinforce or radically alter preconceived views on a future area of study, a career or on life generally. One returning Project Trust volunteer had this to say:

Looking back I see my year as an important factor in my successful university career. It taught me self-motivation and a knowledge of the wide world outside the classroom window. I entered university confident that this was what I wanted to do.

Arbeitskreis Freiwillige Soziale Dienst der Jugend

ATD Fourth World

BREAK

Camphill Village Kimberton Hills

The Camphill Village Trust

Camphill Village USA Inc

Cecil Houses

Centro Studi Terzo Mondo

Churchtown Farm

Community Service Volunteers

The Corrymeela Community

Föreningen Staffausgården

Frontiers Foundation/Operation Beaver

GAP Activity Projects (GAP) Ltd

The Girl Guides Association (UK)

Glasgow Simon Community

Great Georges Project

Health Projects Abroad

Homes for Homeless People

Indian Volunteers for Community Service

Innisfree Village

International Christian Youth Exchange

Internationaler Bund für Sozialarbeit

Involvement Volunteers

Joint Assistance Centre

Lanka Jathika Sarvodaya Sangamaya (Inc)

The Leonard Cheshire Foundation

Loch Arthur Village Community

The Ockenden Venture

The Project Trust

The Simon Community

Simon Community (Ireland)

Sue Ryder Foundation

Universities' Educational Fund for Palestinian Refugees (UNIPAL)

ARBEITSKREIS FREIWILLIGE SOZIALE DIENST DER JUGEND

The Bundestutor, Arbeitskreis Freiwillige Soziale Dienst der Jugend, Stafflenbergstraße 76, W-7000 Stuttgart 1, Germany

Throughout Germany

A Christian organisation coordinating the Voluntary Social Year throughout Germany, aiming to help society, develop Christianity and widen the experiences of the volunteer through practical work and discussions

Young people are invited to work voluntarily in a social institution such as a hospital, a home for old people, or a home for the handicapped. Volunteers become members of a group, planning and evaluating their work together.

Ages 17-25. Applicants should be prepared to participate fully in their placement by working and learning with others, and be sound in body and mind. Experience and qualifications not always necessary. Spoken German essential.

1 year, beginning August, September or October

Board, lodging, DM300 per month pocket money and insurance provided. Five weeks holiday per year.

Recruitment all year

ATD FOURTH WORLD

The General Secretary, ATD Fourth World, 48 Addington Square, London SE5 7LB

Africa: Burkina Faso, Central African Republic, Ivory Coast, Madagascar, Mauritius, Reunion, Senegal
Asia: Philippines, Thailand, Sri Lanka
Europe: Belgium, Britain, France, Germany, Luxembourg, Netherlands, Spain, Switzerland
Latin America: Guatemala, Haiti, Honduras
North America: Canada, United States

An international human rights organisation founded in 1957 in France. Aims to explore all possibilities of partnership with the most disadvantaged families who constitute the Fourth World and to encourage private citizens and public officials to join this effort.

Volunteers spend time at ATD's international centre in France before becoming part of a team. Volunteers run programmes in the heart of very poor communities, building on the strengths and hopes of these families. They provide a forum for the disadvantaged and ensure that the voice of the Fourth World is heard at local, national and international levels. Those interested in becoming long-term volunteers can find out more about the organisation through working weekends, international workcamps or summer street-library programmes.

Ages 18+. There are no professional or academic requirements; everyone is welcome. Applicants should have a genuine interest in learning from the experiences and hopes of very disadvantaged communities as a vital first step to building a future with them, and a willingness to work hard with others in a team.

After a 3 month placement volunteers who want to stay on are expected to make a 1 or 2 year commitment

Volunteers are required to pay their food expenses for the first month; for the following 2 months food and accommodation is provided. People who stay on are paid in increments up to the minimum salary which all permanent volunteers receive after 1 year. Accident insurance provided.

Volunteers receive a full introduction into the work of ATD Fourth World

Recruitment all year

BREAK

The Director, BREAK, 20 Hooks Hill Road, Sheringham, Norfolk NR26 8NL

Sheringham (0263) 823170

Norfolk

A charity founded in 1968, providing holidays, short-stay and respite care for handicapped and socially deprived children, mentally handicapped adults and families with special needs.

Volunteers are needed for residential work at two holiday homes at Sheringham and Hunstanton on the north Norfolk coast. Work as care assistants involves helping with the personal welfare of the guests, their recreational programmes and with essential domestic duties. Placements, involving work discussions and practical assessments, can be arranged for those seeking experience prior to or as part of an educational course leading to qualifications for work with children. Recruits 80-100 volunteers annually.

Ages 17+. Applicants should be mature, stable, patient, understanding, conscientious, and able to accept physical and emotional pressures. No previous experience or qualifications necessary. All nationalities considered. Good command of English essential.

2-12 months

Board, lodging, insurance and £20 per week pocket money provided, plus travel expenses within the UK. 40 hour week.

Recruitment all year

CAMPHILL VILLAGE KIMBERTON HILLS

The Administrator, Camphill Village Kimberton Hills, PO Box 155, Kimberton, Pennsylvania 19442, United States

(215) 935 0300

Pennsylvania

An agricultural community based on a 430 acre estate in the rolling hills of southeast Pennsylvania. There is a total population of 130, including some 50 adults with mental handicaps. The community raises vegetables, grains, fruit and meat, and produces milk and cheese from a small dairy herd. All of these products, plus their own baked goods are sold in a farm store on site.

Volunteers are required to live and work as co-workers within the community, working shoulder-to-shoulder with mentally handicapped adults. Work takes place on the farm and in the orchards, in the bakery, store, coffee shop and the administrative office and in expanded-family homes. Some 10-15 volunteers are recruited each year.

Ages 18+. No previous experience or qualifications necessary. Volunteers should have idealism, enthusiasm and an interest in personal growth. **B D PH**

3 months minimum

Board and lodging provided in a Village home. In the first 3 months volunteers receive $50 per month pocket money, after which they may choose to join the community's system of spending flexibly according to the perceived needs of staff and others in the community. Health insurance provided after 6 months, but not travel costs.

Orientation course available during placement

Recruitment all year

THE CAMPHILL VILLAGE TRUST

The Secretary, Camphill Village Trust, Delrow House, Hilfield Lane, Aldenham, Watford, Hertfordshire WD2 8DJ

Watford (0923) 856006

Throughout the UK

A charity founded in 1955 which aims to provide a new and constructive way of life for mentally handicapped adults, assisting them to individual independence and social adjustment within the communities of the Trust. It guides them towards open employment while helping them to achieve full integration within society by providing a home, work, further education and general care. The centres are based on Rudolf Steiner principles.

Volunteers are needed to work alongside the residents in every aspect of communal life at centres where the handicapped can establish themselves, work and lead a normal family life in a social background. There are three Villages offering employment, two town houses for those in open employment, a college, and centres for agriculture, horticulture and assessment. Volunteers work in gardens and farms run on organic principles, in craft workshops, bakeries, laundries, printing presses, and participate in the general life and chores of the community. Special emphasis is placed on social, cultural and recreational life.

Ages 20+. Applicants should have an interest and understanding in work with the mentally handicapped and be prepared to live in the same manner as the residents. Experience not essential, but an advantage. All nationalities considered. Good command of English necessary.

1 year minimum, if possible

Board, lodging, and a small amount of pocket money provided; 1 day off per week

Recruitment all year

CAMPHILL VILLAGE USA INC

Associate Director, Camphill Village USA Inc, Copake, New York 12516, United States

(518) 329 4851

New York State

An international community of 220 people, about half of whom are adults with mental disabilities. Situated on wooded hills and farmland 110 miles north of New York City, the Village includes a farm, a large garden, workshops, a store and 17 houses shared by 4-6 adults with disabilities and 2-4 co-workers.

Volunteers are required to live and work as co-workers within the community, taking part in work on the land, household chores, crafts, worship and cultural activities. 15-20 volunteers are recruited each year.

Ages 18+. No previous experience or qualifications necessary. Volunteers should have an open mind and a willingness to join in and experience community life. PH depending on extent of ability

6 months minimum

Co-workers are provided with board and lodging in a village house, plus $50 per month pocket money. Those staying 12 months receive $300 towards a 3 week vacation. Health insurance provided, but not travel costs.

5-8 hours per week orientation course provided

Recruitment all year, although to participate in training programme volunteers should plan to join in mid September

CECIL HOUSES

The Director & Secretary, Cecil Houses, 2 Priory Road, Kew, Richmond, Surrey TW9 3DG

081-940 9828

London area

A charity and housing association founded in 1926, providing hostels for homeless and rootless women in central London, sheltered hostels for active pensioners in Ealing and Teddington, and residential care homes for the frail elderly in Kew and Teddington. It aims to create caring communities where individuals can mix with others in like circumstances, where they are offered food, warmth and comfort, and where, above all else, they can have a sense of belonging.

A limited number of volunteers are needed to help care for elderly residents and homeless women. Work includes escorting residents shopping, on outings and to out-patients appointments, and generally improving the residents' lifestyle.

Ages 18+. Applicants must be hardworking, conscientious and enthusiastic and should be able to demonstrate charity, care and compassion. No qualifications or direct experience required. All nationalities considered. Working knowledge of English essential.

4+ months

Shared accommodation, all meals and £20 per week pocket money provided. 39 hour week. 1 week's holiday every 4 months

Recruitment all year

CENTRO STUDI TERZO MONDO

The Director, Centro Studi Terzo Mondo, Via G B Morgagni 29, 20129 Milan, Italy

Milan (2) 2719041/2940041

Africa: Angola, Chad, Ethiopia, Mozambique, Somalia
Asia: India, Indonesia
Latin America: Brazil, Ecuador, Peru

Founded in 1962, the Centre has a wide-ranging involvement with the Third World, which includes arranging development projects, organising courses, initiating studies and research, and issuing documentation, books and journals. Also recruits volunteers for other Italian organisations employing volunteers overseas.

Volunteers are needed to work as teachers, in the medical and social services, in community work, and to organise integrated projects. Recruits 25 volunteers annually.

Ages 18+. Applicants should be reliable and have a serious commitment to voluntary work. Qualifications not always necessary but often desirable, depending on the post. All nationalities considered.

Open ended commitment

Board and accommodation depends on the country, but usually provided in private house. $100 per week pocket money and insurance provided. 36 hour week. Travel costs are met for periods of at least 6 months service. Advice given to participants on obtaining sponsorship.

Compulsory orientation course organised for those without qualifications and experience. On return, advice/debriefing meetings organised every two months.

Recruitment all year

CHURCHTOWN FARM

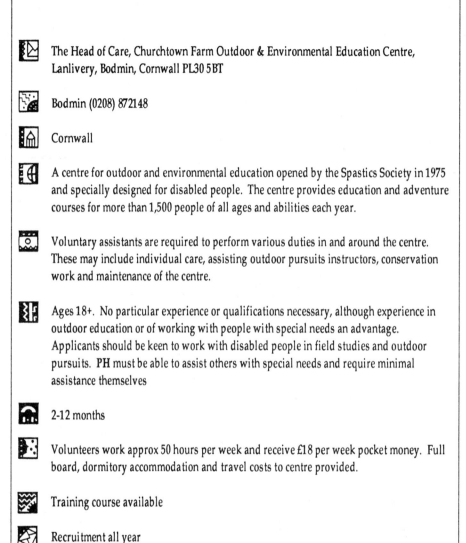

The Head of Care, Churchtown Farm Outdoor & Environmental Education Centre, Lanlivery, Bodmin, Cornwall PL30 5BT

Bodmin (0208) 872148

Cornwall

A centre for outdoor and environmental education opened by the Spastics Society in 1975 and specially designed for disabled people. The centre provides education and adventure courses for more than 1,500 people of all ages and abilities each year.

Voluntary assistants are required to perform various duties in and around the centre. These may include individual care, assisting outdoor pursuits instructors, conservation work and maintenance of the centre.

Ages 18+. No particular experience or qualifications necessary, although experience in outdoor education or of working with people with special needs an advantage. Applicants should be keen to work with disabled people in field studies and outdoor pursuits. **PH** must be able to assist others with special needs and require minimal assistance themselves

2-12 months

Volunteers work approx 50 hours per week and receive £18 per week pocket money. Full board, dormitory accommodation and travel costs to centre provided.

Training course available

Recruitment all year

COMMUNITY SERVICE VOLUNTEERS

 Volunteer Programme, Community Service Volunteers, 237 Pentonville Road, London N1 9NJ

 071-278 6601

 Throughout the UK

 A national volunteer agency which invites all young people to experience the challenge, excitement and reward of helping people in need. For over 30 years CSV has seen the unique contribution that volunteers make to the lives of those they help.

 Over 2,000 volunteers are placed each year in some 600 projects throughout the UK. Volunteers work with elderly people, physically handicapped children and adults, young people in care or in trouble and people leaving hospital. Volunteers are placed according to their interests, personality, experience and the needs of the project; work is usually with individuals or small groups, not in large institutions. Project examples include independent living projects which enable individuals or families with personal difficulties or disabilities to live in their own home; volunteers help them with domestic chores and personal care, and may accompany them to work or college, or to restaurants or cinemas. Volunteers also work in group homes for people who may have a learning difficulty, who are leaving care, or who are recovering from mental illness. Volunteers help residents to lead their own lives as fully as possible by helping them with personal care and to shop, plan meals and enjoy leisure and social activities. Some placements are in hostels for homeless young people. Volunteers help with administrative tasks and housework, and spend time befriending residents, talking and listening to them and helping them find accommodation, employment or claim benefits.

 Ages 16-35. Applicants should have enthusiasm, energy and a commitment to helping others. No academic qualifications or previous experience necessary. B D PH

 4-12 months

 Volunteers are placed away from their home area. Full board, accommodation and £20 weekly allowance provided. 40 hour week. Overseas volunteers pay £395 placement fee.

 Each placement is reviewed after 1 month, and CSV staff liaise with the volunteer and project organiser throughout the placement. One person on every project is assigned to the volunteer for support and regular supervision.

 Recruitment all year; placements take 6-8 weeks to arrange

THE CORRYMEELA COMMUNITY

 The Volunteer Coordinator, The Corrymeela Community, Ballycastle, County Antrim, Northern Ireland

 Ballycastle (026 57) 62626

 Northern Ireland

 Founded in 1965, Corrymeela is an open village situated on the north Antrim coast, comprising a house, cottages and youth village, and supported by the Corrymeela Community, a group of people drawn from many different Christian traditions who work for reconciliation in Northern Ireland in many different conflict situations and promote a concern for issues of peace and justice in the wider world. People under stress, such as those from problem areas, families of prisoners, the disabled and many others, go to Corrymeela for a break or holiday; conferences and other activities challenge participants to look critically at contemporary issues.

 A limited number of volunteers are needed to participate in the programme work of the residential centre, working with the groups who use the centre and being the link during their stay. They should expect to be involved in the practical aspects of running the establishment, assisting with catering arrangements, preparing accommodation, and working in the kitchen, laundry or reception.

 Ages 19+. No qualifications or experience necessary. All nationalities considered. Applicants must be fit and adaptable to cope with the demands and pressures of community life and a very busy programme, and have a commitment to the process of reconciliation.

 1 year, starting September

 Accommodation in shared private study bedrooms with all meals, £20 per week pocket money and insurance provided. Travel grant of £75 for volunteers from outside Ireland. 40-60 hour week. 6 days free per month; 1 week's holiday for every 3 months service.

 Prospective volunteers should spend a few days at Corrymeela before applying. Weekly briefing and reflection programme with the full-time volunteer coordinator. Great care is taken in terms of staff support, external consultancy and pastoral access.

 Apply December-March

FÖRENINGEN STAFFAUSGÅRDEN

The Director, Föreningen Staffausgården, Box 66, Furugatan 1, 82060 Delsbo, Sweden

0653-16850

Delsbo

A Camphill Village consisting of a training school for adolescents with mental handicaps and a nearby farm for handicapped adults. The community also has a garden, a bakery, three family houses, and workshops for weaving and woodwork.

Co-workers are required to live and work with mentally handicapped people, playing a full part in Village life including domestic tasks, crafts and farmwork.

Ages 19+. No previous experience or qualifications necessary, but applicants must have a strong desire to share a period of their life with handicapped people. Applicants should be willing to learn Swedish; courses are provided. **B D PH**

6 months minimum; 1 year preferred

Co-workers receive board and lodging in a Village home shared with 10-15 other people, plus pocket money to cover their immediate needs. Accident and health insurance provided. Ticket home paid after 6 month stay.

Training seminars and courses organised in arts, therapy and the philosophy of anthroposophy

Recruitment all year

FRONTIERS FOUNDATION / OPERATION BEAVER

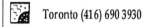

The Program Coordinator, Frontiers Foundation/Operation Beaver, 2615 Danforth Avenue, Suite 203, Toronto, Ontario, M4C 1L6, Canada

Toronto (416) 690 3930

Alberta, Ontario and Northwest Territories, Canada

Works in cooperation with requesting communities to fulfil their needs for basic housing. Volunteers from all over the world participate in the programme to make practical efforts to reduce poverty and to meet people from culturally diverse backgrounds. The Foundation also runs recreation programmes providing stimulating, creative alternatives to the boredom and social problems endemic in many Native American communities.

About 80% of volunteers work on practical projects in cooperation with Native and non-Native peoples in rural communities in Ontario, Alberta and Northwest Territories. Construction projects involve building or renovating wood frame or log houses. Recreation volunteers work in Alberta with local youth workers organising games, camp-outs and other activities for the youth of the community during the summer months.

Ages 18+. Applicants should be hardworking, open-minded, flexible and culturally sensitive. They must also be able to live without television, flush toilets, and in some cases without running water or electricity. Volunteers with construction skills are given first priority, and previous voluntary experience is an asset. For recreation projects applicants should have experience of working on camps or with children.

12+ weeks (16+ weeks for Northwest Territories), beginning April-October; most volunteers arrive for the summer session, June-August. Service can be extended for up to 18 months, depending on performance in first period.

Salary not provided initially; modest living allowance paid after 12 week minimum period. Accommodation, food, local travel expenses and insurance provided. Travel to Canada and to the orientation site (Toronto or Edmonton) is the volunteer's responsibility.

Volunteers receive detailed information in the application kit. Summer session volunteers are involved in an intensive 2-day orientation, while volunteers for other months participate in a less formal 1-day orientation.

Apply at least 3 months in advance; recruitment all year

GAP ACTIVITY PROJECTS (GAP) LTD

The Company Secretary, GAP House, 44 Queen's Road, Reading, Berkshire RG1 4BB

Asia: Hong Kong, India, Japan, Malaysia, Nepal, Singapore
Europe: Bulgaria, France, Germany
Latin America: Ecuador, Mexico
Middle East: Israel
North America: United States

A charity founded in 1972 to give those with a year between leaving school and going on to further/higher education or vocational training the opportunity to work in another country

Social work attachments are available in orphanages, homes for the elderly, hospitals, children's homes, or working with youth groups or physically handicapped people. Participants work as general assistants, providing help and care. Many of the projects can be physically and emotionally demanding.

Ages 18-19. UK nationals only. Applicants should be reliable, possess initiative and intelligence, and be prepared to work hard. Those working on French, German or Latin American projects must be able to speak the relevant language.

Most placements are for 6 months; some for 9-12 months

Board and accommodation provided, and usually a small amount of pocket money. Volunteers must find their own travel and insurance costs, plus the placement fee of £150-£300, depending on country chosen.

Candidates attend a briefing session before departure

Apply early in September of last year at school. Interviews held November-March.

THE GIRL GUIDES ASSOCIATION (UK)

The International Secretary, Girl Guides Association, 17-19 Buckingham Palace Road, London SW1W 0PT

071-834 6242

India, Mexico, Switzerland, Britain (London)

The Girl Guides Association of the United Kingdom, founded in 1920 by Robert Baden Powell, is a voluntary organisation for girls. It gives them the opportunity to follow any number of interests and at the same time learn self-reliance and self-respect. Guides share a commitment to a common standard set out in the Promise and Law.

Volunteer work is available in London and overseas at centres owned by the World Association of Girl Guides and Girl Scouts. Projects may include assisting the development of Guide Associations, training adult leaders or administration duties in connection with Guide House. The work is sometimes strenuous and the hours long.

Ages 18+. Qualifications and experience required vary according to the position. Volunteers must be members of the Association. B D PH considered

Variable

Board, accommodation and pocket money provision vary according to the position. Insurance provided in some cases. Travel costs usually paid by the volunteer. Advice is given to participants on obtaining sponsorship. Members are encouraged to write articles for the magazines on their return.

Recruitment all year

GLASGOW SIMON COMMUNITY

Volunteer Coordinator, Glasgow Simon Community, 133 Hill Street, Garnethill, Glasgow, G3 6UB

041-332 3448

Glasgow

Aims to offer time, friendship, practical help and supportive accommodation to men and women who have been homeless for some time

Volunteers work in an outreach team in 5 small group homes where residents and volunteers live together, sharing in the running and day-to-day life of the community. Contact is made with homeless people, especially rough sleepers, and friendship and practical help are offered.

Ages 18+. No academic qualifications required. Experience useful but not essential. Volunteers should have a non-patronising attitude, the ability to accept people for what they are and to cope with stress and emotional pressures. PH

6+ months

5 day week, 24 hour day. Volunteers receive £15.70 per week plus £18.63 per week compulsory savings which is paid in lump sum at end of placement. £40 shoe allowance per year. £53.75 for 10 day holiday every 3 months. Full board accommodation provided with separate accommodation for days off.

Informal one-to-one training provided during the first month, with training visits to relevant agencies. Regular opportunities to participate in training events and attend conferences.

Recruitment all year

GREAT GEORGES PROJECT

 The Duty Officer, Great Georges Project, The Blackie, Great George Street, Liverpool 1

 051-709 5109

 Liverpool

 Founded in 1968, the Great Georges Community Cultural Project, known locally as The Blackie, is a centre for experimental work in the arts, sports, games and education of today. It is housed in a former church in an area typical of the modern inner-city: multi-racial, relatively poor, with a high crime rate and a high energy level, but sometimes a lot of fun. The project sets about its task of building bridges between the artist and the community with great enthusiasm, offering a wide range of cultural programmes, workshops and exhibitions, including pottery, sculpture, printing, film/video making, photography, painting, writing, outdoor plays, carpentry, puppetry, playstructures, music, mime and dance. Open 7 days a week, 10.00-24.00.

 Volunteers are needed to work with children/adults in projects undertaken at the Project and in the local community, with endless opportunities to learn and create. The general work of running the Project is shared as much as possible, with everyone doing some administration, cleaning, talking to visitors and playing games with the children. Recruits 100-150 volunteers annually.

 Ages 18+. Applicants should have a good sense of humour, stamina, a readiness to learn, and a willingness to work hard and share any skills they may have. The children/young people who visit the Project are tough, intelligent, friendly and regard newcomers as a fair target for jokes, so the ability to exert discipline without being authoritarian is essential. No direct experience required. All nationalities considered. Good working knowledge of English needed.

 1+ months. Volunteers are particularly needed at Christmas, Easter and summer.

 Accommodation in shared rooms at staff house; long-term volunteers may have own room. Vegetarian breakfast and evening meal provided; cooking on a rota basis. Those who can afford to, contribute approx £15 per week to cover food and housekeeping. Wages generally paid after 6 months. 12 hour day minimum, 6 day week.

 Orientation course includes a talk with films and a pack of Project literature

Recruitment all year

HEALTH PROJECTS ABROAD

The Director, Health Projects Abroad, HMS President (1918), Victoria Embankment, London EC4Y 0HJ

071-583 5725

Developing countries; most recently Cameroon and Tanzania

A charity registered in July 1990 which aims to provide logistical, technical and material support to health authorities in developing countries and the voluntary and non-governmental organisations that are working with them; and to give young people and qualified personnel the opportunity to participate in projects and learn first hand about the realities of life in a developing country.

Volunteers work alongside local people, helping to complete projects. They are usually involved in simple tasks such as assisting with the construction of new dispensaries and renovation work at health centres and hospitals. They work with local people under the guidance of volunteer professional engineers and medical staff.

Ages 18-28. Applicants must have enthusiasm and energy, be open minded and receptive to change, sensitive to the needs of the host community and able to work as part of a team. No specific skills, qualifications or experience required. B D PH all applicants considered on an individual basis

3 months, beginning June and September. Volunteers are allowed 2 weeks travel time at the end of each project.

Each volunteer is required to raise £2,250 towards the cost of their own participation. This covers travel, accommodation, food, medical insurance and support for the project. Advice is given on raising funds.

Applicants are selected at an assessment and briefing weekend. Two compulsory training weekends are held before departure and a debriefing weekend is held 4-5 weeks after volunteers return.

Apply by late September for June departure; by mid November for September departure

HOMES FOR HOMELESS PEOPLE

The Volunteer Recruitment Officer, Homes for Homeless People, Smithfield House, Digbeth, Birmingham B5 6BS

021-622 1502

Throughout the UK

Founded in 1969, an association of local groups running day centres, night shelters and residential houses for single homeless people throughout the UK. The groups believe that residents should be accepted as they are, rather than as society would like them to be. Centres are run democratically by the workers and residents, with everyone sharing in decision making.

Volunteers are required to help in the day-to-day running of the centres, working out arrangements for cooking, cleaning and shopping, ensuring that decisions are reached within the house to deal with any problems that arise, maintaining house rules and creating a stable and homely atmosphere.

Ages 18+. No experience or qualifications necessary. All nationalities considered. Fluent English essential. Applicants should have a caring attitude and an ability to live and work with fellow volunteers, welding the group together and building the community. They must be able to cope with the physical and emotional pressures of community living and have the confidence to take responsibility.

6-12 months

Terms and conditions of work vary according to the project. Board, lodging, pocket money and insurance are usually provided.

Recruitment all year

INDIAN VOLUNTEERS FOR COMMUNITY SERVICE

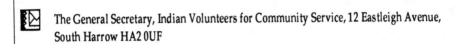

The General Secretary, Indian Volunteers for Community Service, 12 Eastleigh Avenue, South Harrow HA2 0UF

081-864 4740

India

A registered charity founded in 1981 which involves young people in community service, providing them with the opportunity to discover and understand another culture and enabling them to perceive the causes of conflict and disparity in society. Provides orientation, advice and information on visiting rural areas in India and organises seminars and conferences on the issues of sustained development, aid and interdependence, especially in the context of the relationship between the Indian subcontinent and Britain.

Volunteers can help in rural development projects usually in the following areas: helping children in a school or a nursery; repairing small farm machinery in workshops; helping in a health centre; typing, compiling reports and newsletters; and teaching English to children and teachers. The work involves living and working with local people who respond positively to human values.

Ages 18+. Applicants should have imagination and plenty of commonsense. They should be willing to learn from a different culture, have respect for it and value the experience. They must not be demanding or paternalistic, and should be prepared to work hard at anything to improve the quality of life. No qualifications, skills or experience are necessary. Any nationality may apply.

Normally 6 months, leaving September-December and returning March-June

Basic shared accommodation and food provided in village. Participants pay all their travel costs and personal expenses.

Compulsory interview and orientation organised before placements. Guidelines for preparation, advice on travel and health and meetings with returned volunteers are arranged for members only. Membership fee £10 annually; life membership £50.

Recruitment all year

INNISFREE VILLAGE

The Volunteer Coordinator, Innisfree Village, Route 2, Box 506, Crozet, Virginia 22932, United States

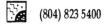

(804) 823 5400

United States

Innisfree's goal is to provide a lifetime residential facility for adults with mental disabilities. The staff consists of volunteers who life and work together with mentally disabled co-workers in a natural and humanistic environment.

Acting as houseparents and co-workers, volunteers are needed to work on the 600 acre farm in the foothills of the Blue Ridge Mountains with the choice of working in the bakery, weavery, woodshop, garden or free school. There are also group homes and supervised apartments in the nearby city of Charlottesville, where volunteers work in the pottery. Recruits 18-20 volunteers annually.

Ages 21+. Volunteers need energy, enthusiasm, patience, and a willingness to work with the differently abled. They must be in excellent health, and interested in the community process in a very rural setting. Volunteers must be college graduates or equivalent, preferably with some experience of working with mentally disabled, recently brain injured or emotionally ill people. Craft skills greatly appreciated. All nationalities considered. Fluent English required.

Volunteers are sponsored under the International Exchange Visitors Programme for 1 year minimum, and have J-1 visa status.

Volunteers have their own room and board in a house of 6-14 people. $150 per month spending money, $100 Christmas bonus, medical insurance and up to $250 for dental expenses provided. Travel costs are paid by the volunteer. Volunteers work a 5 day week, with 2 consecutive days free. Annual holiday entitlement of 21 days, with an additional holiday allowance of $30 per day.

The first month is a mandatory trial period with four orientation sessions covering a brief history of the village and its guidelines, and volunteers are encouraged to get to know the village as well as possible before settling down in one house. At the end of this period, the community evaluates and decides the best placement for the volunteer.

Recruitment all year

INTERNATIONAL CHRISTIAN
YOUTH EXCHANGE

Programme Executive, International Office, International Christian Youth Exchange, Goethestraße 85-87, 1000 Berlin 12, Germany

Africa: Ghana, Liberia, Nigeria, Sierra Leone.
Asia-Pacific: Australia, India, Japan, New Zealand, South Korea.
Europe: Austria, Belgium, Denmark, Finland, France, Germany, Iceland, Italy, Norway, Sweden, Switzerland
The Americas: Bolivia, Brazil, Colombia, Costa Rica, Honduras, Mexico, United States

An international youth organisation established in 1949 as an initiative for reconciliation. It is made up of autonomous national committees based in 28 countries. Independent of any individual church affiliation, it cooperates with national councils of churches, youth movements and international organisations to build up an exchange programme as a tool for peace and justice.

Exchange programme provides the opportunity for young people to live with a family and attend secondary school or, for those over school age, be involved in voluntary social work. Projects may include childcare, assisting the elderly, drug rehabilitation, rural and health development projects, women's groups, peace education and ecological activities. Some 500 young people around the world take part each year.

Ages 16-28. Applicants should be prepared to accept the challenges of living in a different environment amongst people from another culture. They should be able to give and take, think and act towards the future, and be concerned with questions of peace and human liberation.

6 months, beginning January or July; 12 months beginning July/August

Precise terms, conditions and costs depend on the national committee arranging the exchange. Participants are usually expected to pay for travel and insurance, plus a fee to cover accommodation, placement, pocket money and administration.

Orientation, language training and evaluation conference provided by national committee

There is no national committee in the UK; those interested should write for further information to the international office

INTERNATIONALER BUND FUR SOZIALARBEIT/JUGENDSOZIALWERK eV

 Freiwilliges Soziales Jahr, Ludolfusstraße 2-4, D-6000 Frankfurt am Main 90, Germany

 Frankfurt (069) 28 21 71

 Throughout Germany

 An independent, non-profitmaking organisation whose objective is to enable people to integrate into the community, take on personal responsibility and contribute actively to the development of society. They also aim to stimulate people's willingness to participate in voluntary social service, and to develop and improve international understanding and cooperation.

 Operate a Voluntary Social Year programme whereby young people work in various social facilities such as hospitals, old people's homes, sheltered workshops and psychiatric hospitals, assisting in all duties which a non-skilled helper is able to perform, such as helping patients to wash and dress themselves, feeding them and running errands.

 Ages 18+. No previous experience necessary, however applicants should have some knowledge of German.

 6 or 12 months, beginning April (6 months) or September (12 months)

 Participants receive approx DM200 per month pocket money and full board accommodation on site, with cash compensation during days off for meals not provided. 24 days leave allowed for 12 months' service. 40 hours per week, which may include morning/afternoon shifts and weekend duty.

 Week-long briefing seminar held at beginning of service, where participants meet their group leaders and are assigned to their place of work. Further compulsory training courses are held throughout the period of service.

INVOLVEMENT VOLUNTEERS

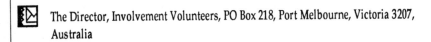

The Director, Involvement Volunteers, PO Box 218, Port Melbourne, Victoria 3207, Australia

Melbourne (3) 646 5504

Australia, Fiji, India, Thailand, United States (California, Hawaii)

Aims to assist people travelling overseas to participate as volunteers in community-based, non-profitmaking organisations throughout Australia and a growing number of countries en route.

Placements are available to suit local needs and include working with mentally handicapped or disadvantaged children; recreation for elderly people; social welfare related training for volunteer organisations; or working in street medical clinics for the homeless or socially deprived.

Ages 17+. Relevant experience welcome, and sometimes necessary for certain projects. Understanding of spoken English essential.

6-8+ weeks

Cost AU$300. Involvement Volunteers provides advice on placements and arrangements, itinerary planning, meeting on arrival; and in Australia initial accommodation, introductions to banking and a communications base. Discounted internal travel available. Board and accommodation vary according to placement, and cannot always be provided free of charge. Volunteers arrange their own visitor visa, international travel and insurance.

Apply at least 3 months in advance; more planning time recommended if possible

JOINT ASSISTANCE CENTRE

 The Convenor, Joint Assistance Centre, H-65, South Extension 1, New Delhi 11049, India

 Throughout India

 A small voluntary group for disaster assistance working in close liaison with other groups throughout India who run voluntary projects of various kinds.

 Operate a learn-while-you-travel scheme whereby volunteers either do administrative work at centres in Delhi or are placed on short-stay workcamps with groups in other areas to help in environmental activities, agriculture, construction, community work, health and sanitation work, teaching first aid or preparation work for disasters. Specific projects are also organised including work on playschemes, organising fundraising campaigns and exhibitions to increase awareness, and teaching English in a village school near Delhi.

 Ages 18+. Experience welcome but not essential. Applicants should have a personal faith in God, and an open mind towards new beliefs. They should be adaptable to difficult situations and have patience, tolerance, understanding and organisational skills. Conditions are very primitive, and the summers (May/June) are very hot. Only vegetarian food is allowed, and applicants must comply with the no alcohol/tobacco/drugs rule.

 3-6 months commitment preferred

 JAC believes that those fortunate enough to have the opportunities of higher education or travel abroad have benefited from the resources available in their society. Therefore each volunteer is required to make a contribution in order participate in voluntary service, usually £60 per month. Self-catering accommodation provided; volunteers share in all housekeeping duties. Registration fee £10. No travel, insurance or pocket money provided. Volunteers must make their own arrangements for obtaining a visa. Travel within India is paid only if it is on JAC business.

 No prior briefing arranged, but there are opportunities to take part in disaster management programmes and conferences. JAC can also put applicants in touch with former volunteers.

 Apply at least 3 months in advance to Friends of JAC, c/o Mike Hicks, 15 Burkes Road, Beaconsfield, Buckinghamshire HP9 1PB. Enclose a cheque for £2 made out to Friends of JAC to cover administration.

LANKA JATHIKA SARVODAYA SANGAMAYA (INC)

The Director, SSI, Lanka Jathika Sarvodaya Sangamaya (Inc), Damsak Mandira, 98 Ratawatta Road, Moratuwa, Sri Lanka

Sri Lanka

Founded in 1958, the movement is a large, non-governmental people's self-development effort covering nearly 8,000 villages, providing a practical possibility of realising Mahatma Gandhi's concept of a world society where the well-being of all shall be ensured. It aims to create awareness among deprived communities and to mobilise latent human and material potential for the satisfaction of basic needs in a manner to ensure sustainable development and to develop strategies and implement programmes for this concept.

Volunteers are needed mainly on village-level development projects in agriculture, animal husbandry, agriculture-based industry, appropriate technology, economic activities, irrigation, sanitation, house construction, energy conservation and the development of alternative energy sources. Opportunities also exist for teachers in pre-school and primary education, and for the provision of preventive and curative health care including nursing, first aid, nutrition and feeding programmes, health education and rehabilitation.

Ages 21+. A willingness to teach and to learn is the main consideration; applicants should have an awareness of their responsibility to improve human conditions wherever needed and an ability to work in sometimes difficult circumstances. They should also have a commitment to the promotion of peace and international understanding, and to an ideal that leads to the equitable distribution of the world's resources according to need. Skills and experience vouched for by a recognised organisation or individual preferred, but specialised skills are not a priority requirement, and academic qualifications are optional. All nationalities considered.

6 months minimum

Board and lodging provided at a cost not exceeding Rs200 per day, but may be less in outstations. Volunteers are expected to meet their own travel, insurance and living expenses.

Compulsory orientation course organised. End of service evaluation provided, at which the volunteer's subsequent activities and placement in the home country is discussed.

Recruitment all year

THE LEONARD CHESHIRE FOUNDATION

 Secretary to Personnel Adviser, The Leonard Cheshire Foundation, Leonard Cheshire House, 26-29 Maunsel Street, London SW1P 2QN

 071-828 1822

 Throughout the UK

 A charitable trust founded in 1948, with some 200 Homes in 36 countries including over 80 in the UK. It has no boundaries of sex, creed or race, concerned only with the care of severely handicapped people. The common aim of all Cheshire Homes is to provide care and shelter in an atmosphere as close as possible to that of a family home; residents are encouraged to lead the most active life their disabilities permit and to participate in the running of the Home and decisions affecting it. The Family Support Services scheme provides part-time care attendants to help prevent or alleviate stress in families with a handicapped member and enables disabled people to continue living at home.

 Volunteers are needed in many Homes to assist with the general care of residents who require help in personal matters, including washing, dressing, toileting and feeding, as well as with hobbies, letter writing, driving, going on outings or holidays and other recreational activities. Recruits some 80 volunteers annually.

 Ages 18-30. Applicants must have an interest in and a desire to help the handicapped; the work is hard and requires understanding and dedication. Previous experience useful but not essential. Preference generally given to those planning to take up medical or social work as a career. Volunteers must be adaptable, dedicated, hard working, punctual and willing to undertake a wide variety of tasks.

 3-12 months

 Volunteers work a 39 hour, 5 day week. Board, lodging and at least £25 per week pocket money provided. Travel costs paid by the volunteer.

 Recruitment all year

LOCH ARTHUR VILLAGE COMMUNITY

Admissions Officer, Loch Arthur Village Community, Camphill Village Trust, Beeswing, Dumfries DG2 8JQ

Kirkgunzeon (038 776) 687

Dumfriesshire

A Camphill Village community providing a home, work, further education and general care for approx 30 handicapped adults. The Community consists of 5 houses, a farm and a 500-acre estate.

Volunteers are needed to live and work alongside residents in every aspect of life, including bathing, dressing and other personal tasks. Main areas of work are on the farm and in the garden, houses and workshops. Volunteers are also encouraged to take part in the community's cultural, recreational and social activities.

Ages 18+. Volunteers should be caring, enthusiastic and willing to help wherever they are needed. No previous experience or qualifications necessary.

6-12 month commitment preferred. Some short-term placements available in summer, minimum stay 6 weeks.

Full board accommodation provided in the Community, plus pocket money

On-going instruction is given by experienced co-workers, plus formal introductory course sessions on a regular basis

Recruitment all year

THE OCKENDEN VENTURE

The Recruitment Secretary, Ockenden Venture, Ockenden, Guildford Road, Woking, Surrey GU22 7UU

Woking (0483) 772012

Mainly in Britain; limited opportunities in Sudan, Pakistan and Vietnam

A charity founded in 1955, providing home, health and education in Britain and abroad for stateless refugees and casualties of conflict and oppression, especially children. Despite enormous international resettlement programmes there are still over 17 million refugees throughout the world, increasing numbers of whom are unable to find asylum anywhere. As well as concern for child rescue at international level and refugee resettlement, the Venture also provides education, care and rehabilitation for children who are deprived, at risk or in trouble, and long-term care for young handicapped refugees.

Volunteers are needed in the Venture's UK homes to work as general assistants with refugee families and children, and with mentally and/or physically handicapped children/young people, many of whom are refugees. Help is required with gardening, cooking, painting, maintenance and creative activities. Longer term volunteers are required for refugee reception centres. There are also very limited opportunities for field work with refugees in Sudan, Pakistan and Vietnam.

Ages 18+. Applicants should have a genuine desire to help, a willingness to work hard, and be physically fit. The houses are run on non-institutional lines in order to create homes, so volunteers are expected to accept a fair share of responsibility at all levels for childcare and domestic work. Qualifications or experience not generally necessary. All nationalities welcome. Fluent English essential.

6 months minimum, preferably 1 year

Volunteers receive full board and lodging, employer's liability insurance and a minimum of £22 pocket money per week. Four weeks holiday per year, pro rata for shorter periods.

Recruitment all year, most volunteers join in August/September

THE PROJECT TRUST

 The Director, Project Trust, Breacachadh Castle, Isle of Coll, Argyll PA78 6TB

 Coll (087 93) 444

 Africa: Botswana, Egypt, Namibia, South Africa, Zimbabwe. Asia: Indonesia, Japan, Pakistan, Thailand. Latin America: Brazil, Honduras. Australia, Jamaica, Jordan

 Founded in 1968, Project Trust is a non-sectarian educational trust sending British school leavers overseas for a year between school and further/higher education or commerce/ industry. Its aims are to enable a new generation to experience life and work overseas, gaining some understanding of life outside Europe, particularly in the Third World, and to place volunteers in a way which is of real benefit to the community.

 Projects are specifically chosen to ensure that volunteers are not taking work from locals. Opportunities include medical work and health lectures in hospitals; caring for leprosy patients; working with deprived, handicapped or homeless children; and assisting in health and community development projects. Recruits 200 volunteers annually.

 Applicants must be at least 17.3 years, maximum 19 years at time of going overseas. They should have initiative, commonsense, flexibility and sensitivity and be physically fit and healthy to cope with the climate and conditions. Open to UK passport-holders in full-time education, taking 3 A levels (or equivalent).

 One year, starting August/September

 Volunteers live in the same type of accommodation as a local worker, with food usually provided. Insurance, travel and £25 per month pocket money paid. Leave is at the discretion of the host country. Cost £2,500 of which volunteers must earn at least £150 by themselves and raise the rest through sponsorship.

 Initial interviews held June-January at a location close to the applicant's home; between September and April successful candidates attend a four day selection course on the Isle of Coll, costing £90 plus travel, and deductible from sponsorship money. The island's few inhabitants play a major rôle in the selection and training of volunteers and this, plus the history of Coll give volunteers an invaluable insight into the conditions to be met overseas. Compulsory training course held in July; candidates learn the rudiments of teaching and are briefed on their project. Two day debriefing course on return.

 Applications open 14 months before proposed date of departure

THE SIMON COMMUNITY

 The Deputy Community Leader, The Simon Community, St Joseph's House, 129 Malden Road, London NW5 4HS

 071-485 6639

 London and Kent

 Founded in 1963, the Community is committed to caring and campaigning for and with the homeless, rootless and all of no fixed abode. Catholic founded and inspired, it aims to put into practice the simple Gospel message, but is ecumenical in action with members of all faiths and none. Residents are men and women, young and old, who have been rejected by society and being without support have slipped through the net of the welfare state, and for whom no other provision exists. A night shelter, community houses and a farm house comprise a tier system enabling residents to find the appropriate level of support at a particular point in time. Provides a long-term caring environment where the individual can regain self respect; emergency stopover provision for the temporarily homeless.

 Volunteers are needed to live and work with the residents of Community houses in London and, at the Community leaders' discretion, at the farmhouse in Kent. Activities include helping residents obtain medical care and social security, referral to other organisations, cooking, fundraising and campaigning, housework, administration, group meetings, night duty, going to rough sleeping sites with tea and sandwiches to make contact with homeless people and helping at a night shelter. Emotionally demanding work, dealing with problems including alcoholism, drug addiction and psychiatric disorders. Workers and residents share in the chores and decision making; of particular interest to those seriously considering social work.

 Ages 19+. Applicants should have a commitment to, and some perception of, the aims and philosophy of the Community, with a willingness to learn and adapt, the ability to relate and respond to people. They must be caring, mature and stable enough to take the burden of other people's problems while retaining their own balance, capable of taking initiatives within the framework of a team, learning to cope with crises. Academic qualifications or experience not essential. All nationalities accepted. Good command of English necessary.

 3 months minimum, 6 months or more preferred

 Workers share the same facilities, food and conditions as residents. Pocket money £12 per week. Average 16 hour day; 1 day per week free. 10 days leave after 3 months.

 Recruitment all year

SIMON COMMUNITY (IRELAND)

The Assistant National Director, Simon Community (National Office), PO Box 1022, Lower Sheriff Street, Dublin 1, Ireland

Dublin (1) 711606/711319

Cork, Dublin, Dundalk and Galway

A voluntary body offering support and accommodation to the long-term homeless at night shelters and residential long-stay houses in Cork, Dublin, Dundalk and Galway. Full-time work in Simon is demanding and involves a very full commitment to people who will be difficult and who will challenge the volunteer's motivation and feelings. It does not suit everyone, but for those whom it does it can be a very rewarding and enriching experience .

Volunteers are required to work full-time on a residential basis, living-in and sharing food with residents, taking responsibility for household chores and working to create an atmosphere of trust, acceptance and friendship by talking and listening, and befriending residents.

Ages 18+. Applicants should be mature, responsible individuals with an understanding of, and empathy for homeless people. Tolerance and an ability to get on with people and work as part of a team are also essential. No experience or qualifications necessary. All nationalities welcome; good standard of spoken English essential.

3+ months; first month is probationary period

Volunteers work 3 days on and 2 days off, with 2 weeks holiday entitlement every 3 months. Full board and lodging on the project provided, plus a flat away from the project on days off. Volunteers receive an allowance of IR£32 per week; insurance provided, but not travel costs.

Training on-site is given by project leaders; formal training courses in aspects such as first aid may also be provided

Recruitment all year

SUE RYDER FOUNDATION

The Administration Officer, Sue Ryder Foundation, Sue Ryder Home, Cavendish, Sudbury, Suffolk CO10 8AY

Glemsford (0787) 280252

Throughout the UK

A charity founded in 1952 with over 80 homes throughout the world, primarily for the disabled and incurable, but also admitting those who, on discharge from hospital, still need care and attention. The aim is to provide residents with a family sense of being at home, each with something to contribute to the common good. Seeks to render personal service to those in need and to give affection to those who are unloved, regardless of age, race or creed. The homes are a living memorial to the millions who gave their lives during two world wars in defence of human values, and to the countless others who are suffering and dying today as a result of persecution.

Volunteers are needed at headquarters and in 24 homes all over the UK. Work includes helping with patients, routine office work, assisting in the kitchen, garden, museum, coffee and gift shop at headquarters, general maintenance and other essential work arising. Experienced volunteers also needed for secretarial work and nursing.

Ages 16+. Applicants should be flexible and adaptable. A keen interest in caring work is desirable. Qualifications or experience not essential, but an advantage; preference given to students or graduates. Doctor's certificate required. All nationalities considered. Good standard of English required.

2 months minimum

Board, lodging and £10 per week pocket money provided

Two week trial period. On the job instruction provided.

Recruitment all year; larger number of volunteers required in summer

UNIVERSITIES' EDUCATIONAL FUND FOR PALESTINIAN REFUGEES (UNIPAL)

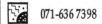

The Volunteer Programme Coordinator, UNIPAL, 3rd Floor West, 9 Cavendish Square, London W1M 9DD

071-636 7398

Israeli-occupied West Bank and Gaza Strip; Palestinian communities in Israel and the Lebanon; occasionally Jordan and elsewhere in the Middle East.

Founded in 1972, UNIPAL is a small educational charity which aims to provide forms of help which will benefit not only individuals but also Palestinian communities and especially over 700,000 refugees still in camps. Palestinian nurses and teachers of English are brought to the UK for training; financial aid is given to Palestinian educational institutions that are helping deprived children and young people; and volunteers are sent to the Middle East to share their skills.

A strictly limited number of volunteers are needed. Work for medium-term volunteers generally involves helping in children's homes and kindergartens; long-term volunteers teach science or English as a foreign language. There are occasional openings for secretaries, physio/occupational therapists, midwives and nurses.

Ages 20-40. Applicants should have sensitivity, tolerance, readiness to learn, political awareness, adaptability and a sense of responsibility. Qualifications and previous relevant experience necessary. Background reading on the Middle East situation essential.

3 months minimum, longer preferred. 1 academic year minimum for teachers.

Food and simple shared accommodation provided. Volunteers serving over 6 months receive fares, insurance and pocket money.

Interviews are held and successful applicants are then briefed on their placement

Recruitment all year

YOUTH WORK/ CHILDCARE

YOUTH WORK / CHILDCARE

Many opportunities exist in a year between to work with children and teenagers outside their family environment, at clubs, playschemes and special centres both in Britain and abroad. The work may include caring for children with disabilities, learning difficulties, emotional or social problems. The opportunities included in this section all last for at least six months. Many short-term opportunities are available during school summer holidays on playschemes or at holiday centres for disadvantaged children. For further details of these see the Children's Projects and Community Work sections in the Central Bureau's annual guide **Working Holidays**.

Organisations recruiting volunteers to work with children and teenagers are looking especially for mature, responsible individuals, usually over the age of 18, preferably with formal or informal experience of similar work. Due to the vulnerability of the group under your care, you will most probably be required to provide detailed references and/or submit your name and address for screening.

Are you genuinely fond of children? This could seem an obvious question, but you may well be living and working with them 24 hours a day. As well as a real liking for kids this requires immense physical and mental energy, patience, and the ability to work hard. Can you exert discipline without being dictatorial? Can you think up enough games and activities to avoid boredom and unruly behaviour? Can you handle having the mickey taken out of your accent, clothes or hairstyle? Do you have the patience and care to help handicapped children to dress, feed themselves or go to the toilet? Can you deal firmly with tantrums, arbitrate between squabblers, comfort someone who is hurt or homesick?

These questions should be considered carefully before you commit yourself to working with children. But don't paint yourself too bleak a picture - the work may be challenging and exhausting but is also tremendously exhilarating. Helping young people discover and develop creative and social skills can prove to be a uniquely rewarding experience.

Au pair work Working as an au pair can be an economic way to spend some time learning the language and experiencing the way of life in another country. Although au pair positions in most countries are now usually open to both sexes, many families traditionally specify females and as agencies recruit accordingly, male applicants will find opportunities more limited. One exception is the au pair programmes in the United States, further details of which are given below.

Government regulations give an au pair the status of that of a member of a family, not that of a domestic. In return for board, lodging and pocket money au pairs are expected to help with light household duties including simple cooking and the care of any children, for a maximum of 30 hours per week. This should allow sufficient time to meet friends, go sightseeing and take a part-time course in the language. Unfortunately, there is no guarantee that these conditions will be met as arrangements depend almost totally on goodwill and cooperation between the host family and the au pair, and au pairs should be aware of these potential problems before accepting a post. The au pair agencies listed below are all reputable and long-standing, and problems such as these are unlikely to occur or will be quickly rectified.

Au pair positions are open to those aged 17-27/30; stays are usually for a minimum of six months. There may be a limited number of short-term summer stays of 2/3 months, depending on the country. The work involves general household chores such as ironing, bedmaking, dusting, vacuuming, sewing, washing up, preparing simple meals and taking the children to and from school, plus general childcare duties. A typical working day is of 5/6 hours, with 3/4 evenings babysitting in a 6 day week. The remainder of the evenings, 1 full day and 3 afternoons per week are usually free. In addition to board and lodging approx £30-£35 per week pocket money is provided. There is usually an agency service charge, and applicants are responsible for their travel and insurance costs, although most agencies can provide information and advice. In some cases, normally after a stay of 12 months or more, the host family will pay a single or return fare. As a general rule, those wishing to work as au pairs should enjoy working with children, have experience of doing housework and at least a basic knowledge of the relevant language.

The au pair programmes in the United States are open equally to males as well as females, ages 18-25, with the emphasis as much on community involvement as on childcare. Character references and a medical certificate are required, and you will also need to have some childcare experience and, particularly as some of the communities are rural, be able to drive. Au pairs work a 5-9 hour day, 5½ day week with 1 weekend free each month. The day is made up of up to 6 hours of active duties including feeding and playing with children, and 3 hours of passive supervision including babysitting. Positions last 12 months. The return flight plus approx $100 per week pocket money, board and accommodation, $300 for a course of study, 2 weeks holiday, and opportunities to travel are provided. Most agencies organising au pair placements in the United States will ask for a good faith deposit of up to £500, which is refunded on completion of the contract. Some agencies can also arrange positions in

Australia and Canada. These are usually for mother's helps and nannies, which are governed by different employment and entry regulations; further details are given below.

Under current regulations au pair agencies in the UK must be licensed by the Department of Employment, and can charge up to a maximum of £47 for finding an au pair position provided that they use an agent abroad as an intermediary. This fee is payable only after the applicant has been offered and accepted a position. It is the responsibility of the agency to ensure that the correct arrangements are made for entry into the chosen country; however it is wise for applicants to check these requirements themselves with the relevant consulate. Applicants should ascertain who is responsible for making travel arrangements and paying the fares; usually agencies will give advice on travel, but applicants make their own arrangements and pay the costs. It is essential to have sufficient funds to pay the fare home in case of emergency. Before leaving au pairs should make sure they have a valid passport, a visa/work permit as necessary, and a letter of invitation from the host family, setting out details of the arrangements that have been made, including details of pocket money and any contributions that may be payable to national insurance or other schemes in the destination country.

Au pair posts should not be confused with regular domestic employment, posts as nannies or mother's helps, or posts advertised as demi pair or au pair plus, which are covered by different employment and entry regulations. Nannies usually have to have undergone formal training, and hold NNEB qualifications or equivalent. They have sole charge of any children, and as a rule, they live with the family, working full-time. Mother's helps work alongside mothers, caring for children, and perhaps doing some cooking and housekeeping. They generally work a 8 hour day, 5/6 day week, and are expected to have considerable childcare experience.

The Au Pair and Nanny's Guide to Working Abroad £5.95, is a comprehensive guide for those considering au pair, nanny or domestic work. Published by Vacation Work, 9 Park End Street, Oxford OX1 1HJ ✆ Oxford (0865) 241978.

The five au pair agencies listed below are just some of the many operating in Britain. The countries in which they make au pair placements are given in *italics*. A wider selection together with comprehensive details can be found in **Working Holidays**, the Central Bureau's complete international guide to seasonal job opportunities, updated annually.

Anglia Agency 70 Southsea Avenue, Southend-on-Sea, Essex SS9 2BJ
✆ Southend-on-Sea (0702) 471648
Australia, Belgium, Canada, Denmark, France, Germany, Greece, Italy, Israel, Spain

Avalon Agency Thursley House, 53 Station Road, Shalford, Guildford, Surrey GU4 8HA
✆ Guildford (0483) 33732
Belgium, Canada, Denmark, France, Germany, Israel, Italy, the Netherlands, Spain, United States

Selective Au Pair Bureau 47 Hindes Road, Harrow, Middlesex HA1 1SQ
✆ 081-861 0858
Austria, Belgium, Canada, Denmark, France, Germany, Italy, Spain

Students Abroad Ltd 11 Milton View, Hitchin, Hertfordshire SG4 0QD
✆ Hitchin (0462) 438909
Austria, Belgium, Canada, France, Germany, Greece, Israel, Italy, the Netherlands, Spain, Switzerland, United States

Universal Care Chester House, 9 Windsor End, Beaconsfield, Buckinghamshire HP9 2JJ
✆ Beaconsfield (0494) 678811
Austria, Belgium, Denmark, France, Germany, Italy, Spain, Switzerland

Beannachar Ltd

British Forces Germany

Camphill Am Bodensee

Camphill Rudolf Steiner Schools

Camphill Special Schools (Beaver Run)

Club de Relaciones Culturales Internacionales

Edinburgh Cyrenians

Friends of Israel Educational Trust

Happy Acres Educational Field Centre

Los Niños

Nansen Internasjonale Center

Schools' Partnership Worldwide

BEANNACHAR LTD

Elisabeth Phethean, Housemother, Beannachar, Banchory-Devenick, Aberdeen AB1 5YL

Aberdeen (0224) 861825 / 868605

Outskirts of Aberdeen

A Camphill community for further education and training, with the aims of providing meaningful work and a home for young adults with varying degrees of handicap or disturbance

Volunteers are required to help care for students and work with them on a communal basis. Work involves gardening, cooking, building, cleaning, looking after animals, laundry, weaving and woodwork. Volunteers are also expected to participate in other community activities such as folk dancing, drama, festivals, walking, swimming, games and outings.

Ages 19+. Volunteers should be enthusiastic, caring and willing to learn. No previous experience or qualifications necessary. **B D PH**

6-12+ months

Volunteers work a 6 day week and receive £18 per week pocket money, plus full board and lodging in the community. Students and staff live together in 2 large family units.

Recruitment all year

BRITISH FORCES GERMANY

The Chief Youth Service Officer, BFG Youth Service, Education Branch, HQ, British Army of the Rhine, BFPO 140

(010-49) 21 61 47 3176

Northern Germany: Berlin, Bruggen, Gutersloh, Hameln, Hamm/Werl, Krefeld, Lippstadt, Osnabrück, Paderborn, Rheindahlen, Soltau/Munsterlager and Wildenrath (locations may change as a result of reduction of British Forces)

The BFG Youth Service was established in 1969 and provides an organisation and structure for all youth provision in those parts of northern Germany in which British Forces are stationed

Operates a Trainee Youth Worker Scheme to recruit leaders for youth clubs. Particularly suitable for mature young adults wishing to gain full-time professional training, and for newly-qualified youth workers, for whom the work will serve as their Youth Service Probationary Year. Work involves being responsible, under professional supervision, for the leadership of youth clubs with a mixed membership of 100-300 children aged 10-16.

Ages 18-25. Applicants should be socially mature, persuasive and outgoing, capable of working on their own initiative but also with committees and other adults. UK nationals only. Applicants must be single or unaccompanied, and have experience of working with young people. Knowledge of German welcome but not essential.

12 months, beginning August/September

Honorarium of DM6,891 per annum, accommodation and food allowance provided. Trainee youth workers are entitled to 5 weeks annual leave and the use of certain BFG facilities. Hours of work similar to those of youth workers in Britain, including evening sessions and weekend work.

Recruitment normally takes place in late spring

CAMPHILL AM BODENSEE

Sekretariat, Camphill am Bodensee, Heimsonderschule Brachenreuthe, 7770 Überlingen-Bodensee, Germany

(07551) 80070

Near Überlingen

A residential school for mentally handicapped children, based near Lake Constance. The school cares for 90 children aged 4-17, and consists of 10 house communities, a therapy building, a community hall, a garden and a farm. Emphasis is placed on catering for the needs and problems of autistic children. The work is based on the teachings of Rudolf Steiner, and aims to help the children achieve individual independence within the Camphill Trust communities.

Volunteers are required to live and work with the children, helping out in classes and with bathing, dressing and other personal tasks. Volunteers are also encouraged to participate in the cultural, recreational and social aspects of community life.

Ages 19+. No previous experience or qualifications necessary. Volunteers should be caring, enthusiastic and willing to help wherever they are needed. Basic knowledge of German very helpful.

6-12+ months, usually starting mid August

Volunteers work a 6 day week, and have 5 weeks holiday in a year. Full board single/double room accommodation, insurance and DM300 per month pocket money provided. Volunteers pay their own travel expenses.

Those staying for a year have the opportunity to take part in a training course in curative education

Recruitment all year

CAMPHILL RUDOLF STEINER SCHOOLS

Central Office, Camphill Rudolf Steiner Schools, Murtle Estate, Bieldside, Aberdeen AB1 9EP

Aberdeen (0224) 867935

Outside Aberdeen

Founded in 1939 by the late Dr Karl König, the Camphill schools offer residential schooling and therapy, based on the teachings of Rudolf Steiner, for children and young adults in need of special care. Members of staff and their families live with the 185 pupils in 16 separate house communities on the three small estates that comprise the schools' grounds.

Co-workers are required to live with children in family units, helping with the care of children and the running of the house and garden, and of the estate. There are 40-50 vacancies for volunteers each year.

Ages 20-40. No previous experience or qualifications required, but applicants should have an open mind and an interest in children, community life, curative education and anthroposophy.

12 months minimum, beginning August, late October, early January and late April

Co-workers receive board and lodging plus £20 per week pocket money. There is one day off each week, otherwise no separation between on and off duty. Volunteers from mainland Europe are given return fare after 1 year.

1 year introductory course available

Recruitment all year

CAMPHILL SPECIAL SCHOOLS
(BEAVER RUN)

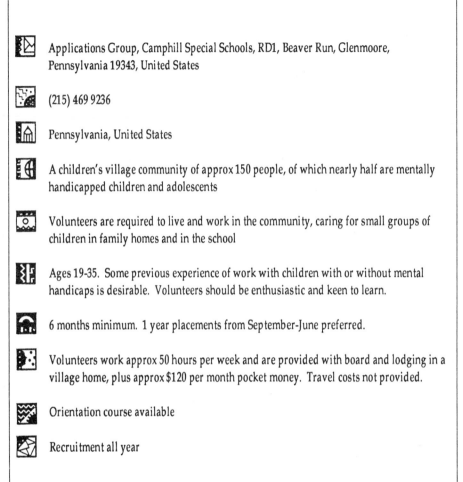

Applications Group, Camphill Special Schools, RD1, Beaver Run, Glenmoore, Pennsylvania 19343, United States

(215) 469 9236

Pennsylvania, United States

A children's village community of approx 150 people, of which nearly half are mentally handicapped children and adolescents

Volunteers are required to live and work in the community, caring for small groups of children in family homes and in the school

Ages 19-35. Some previous experience of work with children with or without mental handicaps is desirable. Volunteers should be enthusiastic and keen to learn.

6 months minimum. 1 year placements from September-June preferred.

Volunteers work approx 50 hours per week and are provided with board and lodging in a village home, plus approx $120 per month pocket money. Travel costs not provided.

Orientation course available

Recruitment all year

CLUB DE RELACIONES CULTURALES INTERNACIONALES

The President, Club de Relaciones Culturales Internacionales, Calle de Ferraz 82, 28008 Madrid, Spain

Madrid (1) 541 71 03

Spain

A non-profitmaking, cultural, educational and linguistic association offering a wide-ranging international programme for young people wishing to broaden their knowledge of foreign languages and cultures

Young people are required to work at hotels in Spanish coastal resorts, looking after children and arranging entertainments for them such as contests and parties

Ages 18-28. Applicants must have patience, imagination and experience of working with children. Knowledge of Spanish essential; other languages also welcome.

1-3 months, April-September

4-6 hour day, with full use of hotel facilities in spare time. Board, lodging, insurance and £40 per week pocket money provided. Registration fee £25.

Apply January-March

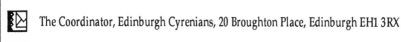

EDINBURGH CYRENIANS

The Coordinator, Edinburgh Cyrenians, 20 Broughton Place, Edinburgh EH1 3RX

031-556 4971

Edinburgh and West Lothian

Set up in June 1968 to develop and provide services to homeless single people, the Edinburgh Cyrenian Trust runs a city community in central Edinburgh and a rural project on a small organic farm in West Lothian. Residents are a mix of young people referred by social workers, hospitals or other agencies.

Volunteers are required to live and work alongside residents and other volunteers, sharing the jobs involved in running a large household, with particular responsibility for managing household accounts, upholding the rules of the community, attending weekly meetings, forming helpful relationships with community members and offering assistance and support to residents. Community life is challenging, difficult and stressful, but can also be extremely rewarding. Some 22 volunteers are recruited annually.

Ages 18-30. Applicants should have personal commitment, open-mindedness, willingness to learn, a sense of responsibility, energy, enthusiasm and a sense of humour. No previous experience or qualifications necessary. All nationalities accepted; working knowledge of English essential. **B D PH** unsuitable for wheelchairs

6+ months

Volunteers work a 5 day week and receive full board accommodation in the community, with access to a flat away from the community on days off. £22 per week pocket money provided, plus £160 grant for 1 week's holiday after 3 months, £30 clothing allowance and £135 leaving grant after 6 months.

Regular training given and volunteers are supervised by non-residential social workers

Recruitment all year

FRIENDS OF ISRAEL
EDUCATIONAL TRUST

The Director, Friends of Israel Educational Trust, 25 Lyndale Avenue, London NW2 2QB

071-435 6803

Israel

Founded in 1976, the Trust aims to promote in the UK a knowledge of Israel and its people via talks, lectures, presentations and working visits to Israel

The scheme offers 12 school leavers a chance to spend time in Israel. The programme involves working in youth centres as part of a community service programme in both rural and urban environments or working on a kibbutz and teaching in high school. Participants take part in seminars, organised tours and independent travel.

Ages 18+. UK nationals only. Applicants should be open to new experiences and want to participate in the pioneering spirit of modern Israel. They should be prepared to undertake any tasks/challenges set. No experience necessary, but most applicants are A level students.

5 months, February-August

Travel, basic lodging, food in canteen or self-catering and basic insurance provided, plus back-up from specialists throughout the programme. Token amount of pocket money provided on the kibbutz. Approx 30 hour week.

Full debriefing given on return, with ongoing contact

Apply by 1 July. Applicants should explain in an essay of minimum 400 words their reasons for wishing to visit Israel, and enclose two references, one academic, one personal. Shortlisted candidates are interviewed.

HAPPY ACRES EDUCATIONAL FIELD CENTRE

Brenda Cauldwell, Director, Happy Acres Educational Field Centre, PO Box 65, Magaliesburg 2805, South Africa

South Africa

A non-profitmaking organisation providing biology courses for children in the Witwatersrand area. Schoolchildren of all races visit daily. There are also residential courses, and holiday camps during school holidays. The Centre is set in grounds near the Magaliesburg Mountains, 1 hour's drive west of Johannesburg and has plant displays in greenhouses and a collection of small mammals, reptiles, insects, frogs and fish.

Recruit 3-4 young people each year to work at the Centre. Staff help care for plants and animals, and work with children, organising games, guided walks and other activities.

Ages 18-25. Applicants should have an outgoing, pleasant personality and the ability to work and live in a group. No special skills or qualifications necessary as on-the-job training is given. GCSE or A level biology useful, and experience of working with children an advantage.

12 months. Staff are encouraged to take time off to tour the country during slack periods.

Staff are given board and lodging at the Centre and a salary of approx R700 per month. They must provide their own insurance and return fare to Johannesburg.

Apply as early as possible

LOS NIÑOS

The Office Manager, Los Niños, 9765 Marconi Drive, Suite 105, San Ysidro, California 92173, United States

(619) 661 6912

United States/Mexico border cities of Tijuana and Mexicali

Founded in 1974, Los Niños is a non-profitmaking organisation providing community development services in the areas of literacy, early childhood education, nutrition, health and family gardens.

Volunteers assist in literacy programmes, the education of small children, agriculture or nutrition projects such as nutrition courses for women and school lunch programmes in kindergartens.

Ages 16+. Fluency in Spanish essential. Applicants should be mature, cross-culturally aware and sensitive to the Mexican culture.

12+ months. Short-term projects also available July-August; workshops held October-May.

Volunteers receive board, lodging and $50 per month stipend. Travel costs not provided.

Orientation provided

Apply at least 6 months in advance; write for application or information on any programme

NANSEN INTERNASJONALE CENTER

Recruitment Officer, Nansen Internasjonale Center, Barnegården Breivold, Nesset, 1400 Ski, Norway

(02) 94 67 15/91

Ski, Norway

Aims to help teenagers with social problems at a relief and activity centre in a renovated farm 25 km south of Oslo. The work is based on total participation and involvement from voluntary staff, permanent staff and residents.

Volunteers work in parallel with permanent staff, and partake in all aspects of farm life including care of animals, daily cleaning and cooking, creative work, hobbies and sports with the teenagers, planning and participating in tours. The work is physically demanding but rewarding. The staff is international; working languages are Norwegian and English.

Ages 22+. Applicants should be mature, practical, motivated, committed to working with children in need of care, and willing to take part in all activities. Experience useful but not essential.

6-12 months, beginning February and August. Limited number of short-term opportunities in summer.

Long working hours on a rota basis, with approx 4 days free per fortnight. Board and lodging plus NKr450 per week pocket money provided. Volunteers arrange their own travel and insurance.

Guidance seminar held at beginning of work period, plus weekly help and guidance from permanent staff

Apply at least 3 months in advance in order to allow time for work permit clearance

SCHOOLS' PARTNERSHIP WORLDWIDE

The Director, Schools' Partnership Worldwide, 1 Catton Street, London WC1R 4AB

Schools' Partnership Worldwide, Westminster School, 17 Dean's Yard, London SW1P 3PB

071-831 1603

South India

An educational charity, partly funded by the Overseas Development Administration, committed to promoting closer contact between the UK educational services and those in the developing world. One of its functions is to provide opportunities for member schools to focus guaranteed funding on overseas schools and projects, in return for which selected school-leavers are able to work in those same countries in the year between school and further education. Some 160 positions are offered each year.

Attachments to various types of institutions catering for disadvantaged children, including orphanages, rehabilitation centres and homes for children with physical or mental handicaps. The pattern of work varies enormously but always involves work with children, such as organising activities or teaching. Attachments are in pairs, ideally of two close friends of the same sex.

Ages 18-21. UK nationals only. Applicants should be expecting to gain high A level grades and must be able to show a real commitment. Relevant experience an advantage, and the abilities to take the initiative and work without supervision are essential. Applicants should also be open to other cultures and resourceful enough to cope with living in a hot climate, possibly under spartan conditions. D PH accepted where practicable

4-5 months, beginning September or January

Priority is given to those applying from member schools; those from non-member schools have to be strongly recommended by their school and will need to raise £600 sponsorship in lieu of the school's subscription. Advice is given on fundraising. Participants pay their own airfare (£500) and £10 per month insurance. Accommodation provided but not pocket money.

Compulsory training and induction course held in London prior to departure; cost approx £60

Early application advised

CHRISTIAN SERVICE

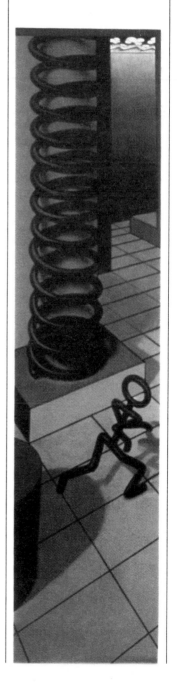

CHRISTIAN SERVICE

The organisations in this section recruit volunteers to work on projects based both in Britain and abroad. Opportunities may involve social service, assisting with the work of churches in their local communities, evangelical outreach work, or a combination of all of these. In general applicants must have a Christian commitment or at least be thinking seriously about their faith. Most agencies will not pry too deeply into an applicant's beliefs as long as it is clear they are happy to share their Christian faith with others. In some cases, however, applicants must be referred by their local church. Volunteers who do not have a Christian faith are likely to find difficulties in relating to the people and community with whom they are working, and are better advised to apply for community and social work placements through other agencies, such as those listed in the Community & Social Service section.

You will need to think carefully about why you feel called upon to do Christian service. Perhaps you want to bear witness to your faith and share it with others. You may be looking for a chance to find out more about your own personal beliefs. You may want to try yourself out for a limited period to see whether you have a calling for a lifetime of Christian service. You may want to discover how Christians live in other countries, or in other parts of Britain, and work in solidarity with them. Or you may feel more motivated to perform a social service by improving conditions for God's people in need. These are some of the reasons why young people choose to serve. Penny Prestage, coordinator of the Time For God Scheme says that applicants are always asked at interview why they want to work as a TFG volunteer:

Many young people want a break from study, or some further experience to test out a future career in youth or social work.

Some are unemployed and for them the year will hopefully act as a stepping stone to future work. Most could fulfil these goals in other kinds of voluntary work, but they also want to serve God and to put their faith into practice.

Mark had been working in a civil service personnel department since leaving school when he applied to Time For God. Working as a volunteer was a chance to express his Christian faith and 'give something back'. He worked in a residential YMCA in London:

The experience opened my mind, I can accept and understand people better now. My faith in Christ has grown much stronger.

Mark is now in the second year of his training to become a youth and community worker, and says this career decision was made directly as a result of his TFG experience.

Jane, now an RE teacher in an inner city area, looks back on her Time For God experience as her first break from home, where she worked with two other volunteers at a church based community centre. She describes it as difficult at times, but invaluable:

In particular, coming to terms with the fact that other volunteers' faith was in some ways very different to my own led to confrontation at times, but also a willingness to step back from views which hadn't been subject to enough reflection, and to respect other traditions and cultures.

She had intended to study chemistry at university but changed to theology and now says the changes in her career plans were good because the previous ones were based on limited self-awareness and were unrealistic.

The accounts above show the influential impact a Time For God year can have on life, work and faith. Penny Prestage feels that there are two particular features of the year which help to give this impact:

*The first is that most volunteers will experience some form of culture shock during the year. This may occur in moving from an urban to rural setting or vice versa, or in living among people of different ethnic backgrounds, or in crossing the North-South divide. This means that to some extent volunteers are vulnerable to their surroundings. They go into an area without the trappings of a particular professional skill and go there to **be** as well as to **do** things. Spending their leisure and work time in the area over a year, they begin to know something of what it is like to belong in those surroundings.*

The second is that TFG offers a network of support and training to help ensure that the experience is fulfilling and challenging but not overwhelming. We visit all placements and check job descriptions and timetables before volunteers arrive and emphasise the need to supply good supervision. There is often an outside support person with whom a volunteer can let off steam and reflect on experiences. TFG itself offers residential training courses at the beginning, middle and end of service, and at least one visit from staff to each volunteer.

The training provides opportunities to meet other volunteers, share experiences and develop skills. All the training events have worship as an important focus for experience. There are Commissioning Services and Re-dedication services held at the events but also volunteer-led worship in small groups. As volunteers come from many different Christian traditions and we encourage participation from all, the worship can be very rich. For some, training events are the most overtly Christian aspects of the year. They may be placed in a residential care home or community centre where only one or two other staff would describe themselves as Christians, or they may spend their time entirely in a Christian community. When placing volunteers we take their preference about this very seriously because for some TFG provides a welcome break from church activities, while for others it is an important chance to be with other Christians.

As the scheme's coordinator, for me the most important part of TFG is the benefit it has for young people. The work they do in placements is extremely valuable, whether that be with people who have learning difficulties, homeless people or children at an after-school club. It will have lasting benefits in itself, but the majority of volunteers leave feeling they have gained far more than they have given. By experiencing life in a different area, volunteers have widened the context of their faith. It is easy to write off people when there is no understanding of them, to shut doors on them because they are 'not one of us'. Volunteers have met and lived with those who are very different from them and yet have felt accepted and accepting. In the future, even in a small way, they can break this mould.

TFG offers opportunities which help prepare young people for more effective Christian service, whatever sphere of secular or church life they enter. Bethan Galliers, a past volunteer now training as a church-related community worker, said:

TFG gave me a vision of being an agent of change in society.

Careforce, a Christian agency that exists primarily to serve churches and Christian organisations throughout Britain and Ireland by placing young volunteers in situations where practical help is most needed, considers a year out to be an opportunity to help whilst free of family and career ties. Careforce has found that a year between spent in Christian service gives those involved a chance to grow, to experience a new situation, and to develop and discover gifts.

The Brethren Volunteer Service, a Christian service programme dedicated to advocating justice, peacemaking and serving basic human needs, recently surveyed 200 of its past volunters to find out the impact on their lives of a period of service. A volunteer service experience is highly individual and unique, and such an experience is difficult to evaluate or put on paper. Nevertheless, over 80% of the respondents claimed that the period of Christian service had given them a better understanding of themselves, helping them to re-examine their opinions and ideas, and strengthening their commitment to serve others. Over two-thirds experienced spiritual growth, bringing them closer to God and the church, strengthening their faith and giving them the courage to stand up for their beliefs. In addition to specific questions, many volunteers took advantage of the opportunity to reply more generally about their experience. Virtually all were united in their opinion that the time spent in Christian service had set a direction for their life by helping to simplify their lifestyle, increasing their awareness of others' needs and clarifying their values.

Apart from the personally enriching experiences gained in a period of service, there is the benefits to those you have served. A pastor on a project in Salta, Argentina, organised under the auspices of Latin Link, wrote to each one of the team's home churches:

I think that you unknown brothers so far away will rejoice to hear about the fruits borne by the young people you sent to our country - fruits of love, kindness, patience and hard work. Besides, they left many doors open to reach people outside the church by their public testimonies through radio, television and the press.

Baptist Missionary Society

Brethren Volunteer Service

Careforce

Christian Foundation for Children & Aging

Christian Outreach

The Church's Ministry among the Jews

Habitat for Humanity Inc

Hothorpe Hall

Interserve

The Ladypool Project

Latin Link

The Leprosy Mission

The Missions to Seamen

Scottish Churches World Exchange

The Time For God Scheme

The United Society for the Propagation of the Gospel

BAPTIST MISSIONARY SOCIETY

John Passmore, Baptist Missionary Society, PO Box 49, Baptist House, 129 Broadway, Didcot, Oxfordshire OX11 8XA

Didcot (0235) 512077

Brazil, France, Jamaica; other countries being considered

An organisation of Baptist churches in the UK, working in relationship with churches overseas

Volunteers are required to work in teams of young people from the UK living, worshipping and working with Christians in other parts of the world. They do practical work with a local Baptist church and get involved with the local community. On their return they share what they have learned with churches in Britain. Three teams of six people are recruited each year.

Ages 18-28. UK nationals only. Applicants must be committed Christians recommended by their own Baptist congregation, seeking the experience of overseas mission. Knowledge of French or Spanish an advantage.

9 months, beginning September, including 1 month's training, 6 months overseas and 2 months on placements with local Baptist churches in Britain. Also run a 3 month summer programme.

Participants contribute up to £950 to travel and training expenses (£250-£800 for summer programmes, depending on placement). Insurance, pocket money and accommodation provided.

Recruitment all year

BRETHREN VOLUNTEER SERVICE

The Recruitment Officer, Brethren Volunteer Service, 1451 Dundee Avenue, Elgin, Illinois 60120, United States

(708) 742 5100

Europe: France, Germany, Ireland, Netherlands, Northern Ireland, Poland, Switzerland. Latin America: Bolivia, Chile, Ecuador, El Salvador, Honduras, Mexico, Nicaragua, Uruguay. Caribbean: Haiti, Puerto Rico, Virgin Islands. China; Egypt; Israel; United States.

A Christian service programme founded in 1948, dedicated to advocating justice, peacemaking and serving basic human needs. BVS is characterised by the spirit of sharing God's love through acts of service and reflects the heritage of reconciliation and service of the Church of the Brethren, its sponsoring denomination.

Over 200 projects, some dealing with immediate needs, others working towards changing unjust systems. Recent projects have needed agricultural workers, environmentalists, maintenance experts, construction supervisors, writers, drivers, cooks, craft workers, medical personnel, childcare aides, social/youth workers, community organisers, instructors to the disabled, aides to the aged, peace/prison reform organisers, refugee resettlement coordinators, teachers and administrators.

Ages 18+. Applicants should be willing to act on their commitments and values; they will be challenged to offer their time and talents to work that is both difficult and demanding. They are expected to study and examine the Christian faith, to be open to personal growth and willing to share in the lives of others. High school education or equivalent required. The programme especially needs those with relevant skills and experience, but also the less experienced if they bring a willingness to grow and a desire to learn. **B D PH**

1 year minimum for United States; 2 years service elsewhere

Participants meet their own costs to orientation in the US; thereafter BVS provides travel, insurance and $45 per month allowance, which may be increased in the second year. Board and lodging provided in apartments/houses or occasionally with a family.

Three week orientation course when the project assignments are made with the input of BVS and the volunteer. There may be a waiting period between orientation and overseas assignment; interim assignments arranged. Debriefing provided during in-service retreat.

Apply at least 3 months in advance

CAREFORCE

 The Organising Secretary, Careforce, 130 City Road, London EC1V 2NJ

 071-782 0013

 Throughout the UK and Ireland

 Careforce is sponsored by the Church Pastoral Aid Society, Crusaders, the Scripture Union and the Universities and Colleges Christian Fellowship. It exists primarily to serve churches and Christian organisations throughout Britain and Ireland by placing young volunteers in situations where practical help is most needed.

 Volunteers work in evangelical churches, mainly in the inner-city, or with evangelical Christian organisations caring for people in need. The range of work includes clerical; cooking and cleaning; maintenance, painting and decorating; visiting, outreach and evangelism; youth and community work; and caring for the disabled or homeless. Recruits approx 80 volunteers each year.

 Ages 18-23. UK and Irish residents only. Applicants should be committed Christians, willing to be placed where they are most needed, to serve and to learn. No previous experience or qualifications necessary.

 10-12 months, beginning September

 Volunteers work approx 40 hours per week. Full board and lodging with a family, in a flat or residential home provided, plus insurance cover. Volunteers receive £18 per week pocket money.

 Compulsory 2 day briefing course organised during first month of placement and halfway through the year

 Apply before the end of July

CHRISTIAN FOUNDATION FOR CHILDREN AND AGING

The Director of Voluntary Service, Christian Foundation for Children and Aging, One Elmwood Avenue, Kansas City, Kansas 66103, United States

(913) 384 6500

Africa: Kenya, Madagascar. Asia: India, Philippines. Caribbean: Haiti, St Kitts. Latin America: Belize, Bolivia, Brazil, Chile, Colombia, Costa Rica, Dominican Republic, El Salvador, Guatemala, Honduras, Mexico, Nicaragua, Peru, Venezuela. United States.

Founded in 1981 by former missionaries and lay volunteers, CFCA is a non-profitmaking, interdenominational organisation dedicated to help overcome hunger, disease, loneliness and suffering by caring for homeless, orphaned, crippled and abandoned children, refugees and the aged. It provides food, shelter, clothing, medicine, education, vocational and nutritional training, and pastoral and social service regardless of age, race or creed.

Volunteers needed include childcare centre workers, health care instructors, nurses, nutritionists, social/community workers, agriculturalists, craft workers, teachers, recreation organisers, house parents, group home staff and secretaries. Support given includes health centres and schools for the poor and handicapped, children's clinics and centres, the training of mothers in vegetable production and for income-producing trades, and educational programmes. Recruit approx 100 volunteers annually.

Ages 21+. Applicants should be motivated by gospel values and a Christian love which calls them to serve the poor, recognizing their dignity and working with them towards self-sufficiency. Some professional skills preferred, although direct experience not necessary. Spanish or Portuguese language skills required for most placements. As part of the screening process, candidates are invited to Kansas City for a discernment period. Applicants will need to cover travel expenses for this. This does not imply that a commitment has been made; rather it is an opportunity for CFCA and the volunteer to find out more about each other before a decision is made. **B D PH**

1 year minimum

Board and lodging provided on site by the host missionary or volunteer. Travel, insurance and pocket money provided by volunteer.

Orientation provided on the mission site

Recruitment all year

CHRISTIAN OUTREACH

The Personnel Officer, Christian Outreach, 1 New Street, Leamington Spa, Warwickshire CV31 1HP

Leamington Spa (0926) 315301

Sudan, Thailand, Cambodia

Founded in 1966, Christian Outreach is a voluntary agency involved in relief work by the provision of primary health care in refugee camps and the support of disadvantaged children in homes.

Skilled volunteers are required to help in children's homes and camps for refugees. Nurses, midwives, nutritionists, engineers, sanitation experts, builders, electricians, mechanics and community development workers are needed. Work includes the operation of mother and child health centres, clinics, community health, community development, education and site maintenance and construction. Conditions can be extremely severe. Recruit 20-25 volunteers annually.

Ages 22+. Applicants should have Christian commitment, a desire to help others and be adaptable. Relevant qualifications required, but previous overseas experience not essential. All nationalities considered. A good command of English necessary.

1 year contract, renewable

Volunteers are housed in local accommodation, with meals prepared by staff. Medical insurance, approx £50 pocket money per month and travel costs provided.

Compulsory orientation course provided

Recruitment all year

THE CHURCH'S MINISTRY AMONG THE JEWS

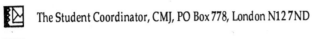

The Student Coordinator, CMJ, PO Box 778, London N12 7ND

081-445 0438

Israel

Founded in 1809 within the Church of England, CMJ aims to take the gospel to the Jewish people, to support and encourage Jewish believers and to teach the Church about its Jewish roots

Volunteers are required to work at CMJ's three centres based in the Old City of Jerusalem, on Mount Carmel near Haifa and in downtown Tel Aviv. Each centre acts as a place of worship, a meeting place and a hostel. The work is mainly domestic and maintenance, with some reception duties.

Ages 18+. Applicants must be fully committed Christians involved in their local church, in good physical and mental health. They will need to prepare themselves for the cultural differences they will face. **B D PH** considered

3-6+ months

Volunteers are provided with full board accommodation in shared bedrooms, and pocket money to meet their needs. They are allowed one day off per week, and holiday time is accrued according to length of stay. Volunteers pay their own travel costs, although home churches may help out with this.

Orientation course held where possible before beginning of placement

Recruitment all year

HABITAT FOR HUMANITY INC

 The Director of Volunteer Services, Habitat for Humanity Inc, 121 Habitat Street, Americus, Georgia 31709, United States

 (912) 924 6935

 Over 400 affiliates in the United States

 An ecumenical Christian housing ministry which aims to provide a decent house in a decent community for God's people in need. This is accomplished by building low-cost homes for sale to poor families at no profit and no interest on a 20 year mortgage.

 Volunteers are needed with construction skills such as carpentry and masonry; office skills such as typing and book keeping; and administrative skills such as fundraising and public relations. Recruits over 100 volunteers annually. Also run projects in 29 developing countries, for which a 3 year commitment is required.

 Ages 18+. Applicants should have a strong desire to house the homeless. Although it is an ecumenical ministry, making no demands on denominational affiliation, applicants should have a Christian commitment. No academic qualifications necessary, but relevant skills required. Experience not always needed, but is an advantage for those considering a long-term commitment. All nationalities considered. **B D PH**

 3+ months

 Housing and utilities provided, plus a small weekly food stipend. Volunteers meet their travel and insurance costs. Advice is given on obtaining sponsorship through denominational agencies, churches and other sources.

 Compulsory orientation course arranged

 Recruitment all year

HOTHORPE HALL

The Director, Hothorpe Hall Christian Conference Centre, Theddingworth, near Lutterworth, Leicestershire LE17 6QX

Market Harborough (0858) 880257

Leicestershire

Founded in 1955 and formerly known as the Lutheran Centre, Hothorpe Hall provides conference facilities for groups of up to 140 people of many different denominations and backgrounds, but mainly from churches, schools and charitable organisations.

Volunteers are needed to look after the guests and maintain facilities. Posts are available as kitchen/domestic assistants. Participation in communal worship, devotions and discussions is expected. Recruits up to 20 volunteers annually.

Ages 18+. No academic qualifications or direct experience needed, but specific skills in areas such as art, music and gardening enable the volunteer to make a valuable contribution to community life. All nationalities considered. Good spoken English required.

6 weeks-1 year

Shared accommodation, all meals, accident insurance and staffroom provided. Pocket money £15 per week. Participants pay their own travel expenses.

Recruitment all year

INTERSERVE

Yvonne Dorey, Personnel Director, Interserve, 325 Kennington Road, London SE11 4QH

071-735 8227

India and Pakistan

A member-society of the Evangelical Missionary Alliance, Interserve is an international evangelical mission with over 400 partners in a wide range of ministry in south Asia and the Middle East, along with several serving among Asian ethnic groups in Britain. It is voluntarily staffed by Christians from both Asia and the West.

Volunteers serve local Christian groups, teaching English, working with computers and caring for children. There are opportunities to learn about missionary work. Recruits seven volunteers per year for its school leaver's programme.

Ages 18+. UK residents only. Applicants must be committed Christians who are involved with their local church/school Christian Union. They should have a good general education to A level standard or equivalent.

7-10 months, beginning October

Volunteers work an average of 30 hours per week, and stay with Christian families or in a hostel. They are responsible for all travel and insurance costs, as well as board and lodging costs and personal expenses whilst on placement.

Compulsory orientation course provided before departure, and personal interview and follow-up at end of placement

Apply as soon as possible, places are limited

THE LADYPOOL PROJECT

Pastor Ralph Mallin, Project Leader, The Ladypool Project, 47 Oakley Avenue, Tipton, West Midlands DY4 0PP

West Midlands

Founded in 1981, an evangelical Christian charity engaged in general social work and providing boating activities for physically and mentally handicapped people. Operates several narrowboats on the canals of the West Midlands, providing outings and holiday facilities for disabled and disadvantaged groups. Other activities include a prayer and visiting service for the seriously ill, and Open Christmas, when food, shelter and a change of clothes are provided for approx 700 tramps, lonely folk and social misfits whilst most of the government's social service centres are closed.

A limited number of volunteers are needed to crew the narrowboats and help out as required on the Project's activities

Ages 17+. Applicants should have a willingness to work and cooperate; a Christian commitment is preferred. Experience with the mentally handicapped useful, but not essential. Applicants must be able to swim and boating experience is useful. All nationalities welcome. Knowledge of English required. **B D PH**

From a few days to a few years

Short-term accommodation and accident insurance provided. Volunteers contribute approx £15 per week towards food. Sponsorship encouraged.

Compulsory 2 day visit prior to appointment to ensure that applicants are compatible with the Project

Recruitment all year

LATIN LINK

 Squadron Leader Michael Cole OBE, Director, Short-Term Experience Projects (STEP), Latin Link, Whitefield House, 186 Kennington Park Road, London SE11 4BT

 071-582 4952

 Argentina, Bolivia, Brazil, Nicaragua, Peru

 Latin Link is a fellowship of personnel in Latin America and elsewhere, who, alongside their supporters and supporting churches, are committed to demonstrating the interdependence of the worldwide church, encouraging cross-cultural mission and channelling resources to and from Latin America for the benefit of the church worldwide

 Short-Term Experience Projects provide a means of allowing young people to work in partnership with the Latin American church, building and extending orphanages, churches, community centres and schools. Projects involve a wide spectrum of tasks and skills, from evangelism through the graphic arts to bricklaying and carpentry.

 Ages 18-35; older applicants with special skills welcomed. Applicants must have a Christian commitment and outlook and a willingness to work as a team with Latin Americans. No previous experience or qualifications necessary, although skills in music or drama, knowledge of Spanish or Portuguese, medical qualifications and practical skills are useful. **B D PH** depending on ability.

 Spring teams: 4 months, mid March-mid July; summer teams: 7 weeks, mid July-September. Spring team members have the option of staying on to join a summer team project.

 Participants are responsible for all travel and living expenses during the project. A rough guide to costs: £1,470 for spring projects, £1,170 for summer projects, covers travel, food, accommodation, insurance and pocket money. Advice given on fundraising. Accommodation is self-catering, and the same as that available to local people.

 Compulsory orientation course held before departure, and reunion conference held in autumn/early winter

 Full details of projects available 3 months before teams are scheduled to depart

THE LEPROSY MISSION

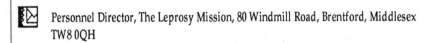 Personnel Director, The Leprosy Mission, 80 Windmill Road, Brentford, Middlesex TW8 0QH

India

A medical missionary society whose main object is to minister in the name of Christ to the physical, mental and spiritual needs of leprosy sufferers, to assist in their rehabilitation and to work towards the eradication of leprosy

The Mission sponsors a limited number of selected medical students to spend an elective period in one of its centres. Students work under the supervision of a medical superintendent, and, as well as gaining an introduction to the treatment of leprosy and the opportunity to observe a general hospital in a tropical setting, they are also encouraged to engage in a special study or project.

Volunteers should be elective medical students in their fourth and final year of studies with suitable training and experience, and who have completed at least 1 full clinical year. They should have a Christian commitment in one of the Protestant denominations, and be considering work in the Third World after qualifying. Letters of recommendation are required from the minister or elder of their church and from the dean of their medical faculty.

8+ weeks

Board and lodging provided. Volunteers pay their own travel expenses.

Volunteers are expected to write a report on their period overseas after returning

Apply at least 9 months in advance

THE MISSIONS TO SEAMEN

 The Deputy General Secretary, The Missions to Seamen, St Michael Paternoster Royal, College Hill, London EC4R 2RL

 071-248 5202

 At some 20 seaports in Britain and around the world, including Brisbane, Dampier, Dunkerque, Fremantle, Hull, Immingham, Kobe, Liverpool, Marseille, Mombasa, New Orleans, Port Hedland, Rotterdam, Seaham, Singapore, Southampton and Yokohama

 An Anglican missionary society founded in 1856, caring for the spiritual and material welfare of seafarers around the globe. The Missions help to combat isolation, exploitation and the dangers of the sea, working for improvements in conditions, education and welfare, serving seafarers of every race, colour and creed, offering a ministry of word, sacrament, counselling care and Christian welcome. The most important feature is the visit of the chaplain and staff to each ship on arrival in port.

 There is a volunteer service scheme for chaplain's assistants, providing an opportunity to be involved in practical Christian service within the shipping industry. Work is varied and involves visiting ships, conducting sightseeing tours, arranging sporting events, visiting hospitals, and helping with worship. Serving in the seafarers' centres can include bar and shop work, arranging video shows, telephone calls, gardening and cleaning. Recruits approx 24 volunteers annually.

 Ages 18-24. Applicants should be sympathetic and understanding, good at quickly establishing relationships, prepared to befriend people of all nationalities and must have an interest in this particular form of ministry. No specific experience necessary, but the possession of a clean driving licence is required. Applicants must be members of a Christian denomination and prepared to participate full in Anglican ministry and worship, and will need three suitable references.

 1 year, starting September

 Board and lodging, travel costs, medical/accident insurance, pocket money and 3 weeks holiday per year provided

 Completed applications should be sent before the end of March

SCOTTISH CHURCHES WORLD EXCHANGE

The Volunteer Programme Coordinator, Scottish Churches World Exchange, 121 George Street, Edinburgh EH2 4YN

031-225 5722

Africa, Asia, Central America, Europe and the Middle East

An agency of the Scottish churches, managed by a committee of representatives or observers from most of the major Christian denominations and a number of missionary societies

Placements are arranged with an overseas partner of one of the Scottish churches or agencies. Volunteers are placed according to their interests, skills and personality, and work on a project from a choice of four areas (AIDS, Women, God's Earth and Witness). Emphasis is placed on volunteers becoming part of the local church and community.

Ages 18+. Open only to candidates from Scottish churches or others in Scotland willing to work in a church-related post. Relevant skills and experience welcome but not essential.

6-18 months, beginning August/September

Food, accommodation and pocket money provided by the host and World Exchange. Volunteers are expected to try and raise at least £1,000 towards the cost of their placement, which represents about one third of the real cost.

Compulsory preparation courses consist of four days at Easter and a week in early summer. On return, volunteers have a medical check, debriefing, and are encouraged to attend a weekend conference for returned volunteers.

Preliminary interviews held October-December; final selection days January-March

THE TIME FOR GOD SCHEME

 The Coordinator, Time For God Scheme, 2 Chester House, Pages Lane, London N10 1PR

 081-883 1504

 England, occasionally Wales

 A charity sponsored by the Baptist Union, United Reformed Church, Congregational Federation, Methodist Association of Youth Clubs, Baptist Missionary Society, National Council of YMCAs and the Church Army, and supported by the Church of England. Offers young people the chance to explore their Christian discipleship in voluntary service.

 Volunteers work in community centres, residential care homes, churches, hostels for the homeless, YMCAs and outdoor pursuits centres. Work can involve arranging activities for youth groups or residents; being good listeners at a community drop-in or at a lunch club for elderly people; visiting people and building up relationships; helping care for physically and mentally disabled children; and helping with typing and administration. Some work in cities, others in rural and suburban areas. Recruits 60 volunteers annually.

 Ages 17-25; overseas volunteers 18+. Applicants should be committed Christians or genuinely searching for a Christian faith, with a concern for others, willing to accept the challenge of Christian service and wish to be involved in God's work in the world. Those with voluntary work experience can be placed in appropriately challenging placements. Volunteers normally recommended by a local church of any denomination.

 6-12 months

 Full board and lodging in private house, staff quarters or self-catering flat, £21 per week pocket money and accident insurance provided. Return fare paid for initial visit and for every 3 months of service. 40 hour week, 1 week's leave after 3 months.
UK volunteers pay £10 registration fee and fare up to a maximum of £10; home church contributes £250 towards training costs (help given where this backing is not available). Overseas volunteers pay £100 registration fee, £250 training costs, travel and insurance.

 3-4 day Preparation for Service Course; Mid-Service Course after 4 months; 2 day End of Service Gathering. The training programme is seen as an essential part of the voluntary service, encouraging reflection on the experience and the linking of faith and action. Volunteers receive support and supervision, and one or more visits during the year.

 UK volunteers should apply 6 weeks-8 months in advance; overseas volunteers 6-12 months in advance, as there is competition for places

THE UNITED SOCIETY FOR THE PROPAGATION OF THE GOSPEL

Short-Term Experience Programmes Officer, Mission Personnel Team, United Society for the Propagation of the Gospel, Partnership House, 157 Waterloo Road, London SE1 8XA

071-928 8681

Many countries worldwide, especially in the Third World

Founded in 1701, the Society enables the Church of England to relate effectively to Anglican churches throughout the world and to support the work of overseas churches by offering them personnel, funding and bursaries

Operates the Experience Exchange Programme, which was established to enable Christians from the UK to learn from the insights and experiences of Christians in other countries. Volunteer placements are agreed by local Anglican bishops and leaders of Christian community projects. The volunteers assist in schools, medical centres, social welfare and agricultural projects. Recruits 20 volunteers annually.

Ages 18-30. Applicants must be mature practising Christians with an interest and commitment in identifying with a local Christian community. They should also be adaptable to new situations, resourceful, sensitive to people and willing to suffer some hardship and loneliness. UK nationals only. No special qualifications or experience necessary.

6-12 months, usually commencing in the autumn

Volunteers pay their fares and insurance, and contribute to board and lodging costs. Advice given on obtaining sponsorship.

Compulsory orientation courses arranged, with advice and debriefing on return home

Recruitment all year

STUDY OPTIONS

The higher education institution you have been accepted for will often expect you to undertake a considerable amount of private study before commencing the course. In many cases it is possible to satisfy these requirements and acquire additional experience through a course of study. The year between offers an excellent opportunity to broaden academic experience beyond your own subjects and at the same time possibly acquire some practical skills relevant to a future career. This section outlines some of the available opportunities including language learning and attending school in another country.

Short courses You may be considering the option of taking a course of study for part or all of your year between. If your examination results are disappointing you may be undertaking a revision course before re-takes. Or perhaps you would like the chance that a course will give you to devote time to a hobby or interest. If you are unsure of what degree course to take or what career to pursue, a short course may help you to make a decision by giving you insight into a specific subject or type of work. Or it may give you experience and qualifications which widen the choices available to you. You may wish to gain a recognised qualification in a certain field, or some vocational training before taking up employment. Or you may decide to gain marketable assets such as computer experience or keyboard skills, which you can put to immediate use earning money to finance the rest of your year between.

There is an enormous variety of short courses suitable for school-leavers or post-graduates; some examples are given below. Your school, careers office or local library should be able to provide more detailed information on where to apply to do a particular course.

Accounting	Marketing/advertising
Administration	Mechanics
Alternative medicine	Media studies
Archaeology	Modern languages
Art & design	Personnel management
Business studies	Performing arts
Communication	Photography
Computer studies	Secretarial skills
Fashion	Social work
Health & beauty	Sports instruction
History of art	Translating/interpreting
IT studies	Travel & tourism
Interior design	Teaching
Journalism	TEFL
Languages	Women's studies
Librarianship	Youth/community work

Unlike first degree and other designated courses, short courses may not qualify for mandatory awards; moreover if you do get a grant it could affect your entitlement later on. At privately run schools, which are likely to offer a greater range of the more special interest courses, you will be expected to pay your own tuition fees. This may not be the case if you opt to do a course in a public sector college, as your local authority may pay the fees for you. Grant and fee-paying entitlements for short courses will vary depending on where you live and where you plan to study. If financial arrangements are likely to be a problem you should check with your local education authority to find out what you are entitled to before committing yourself to any course.

If there is no possibility of getting a grant you may be able to arrange a loan to cover fees and living expenses which you can pay back either during your course if you have the time to take on a job, or afterwards, when you may be able to use your newly-learned skills to earn money.

Language courses A year out presents an ideal opportunity to learn or brush up on a foreign language, perhaps by spending some time studying in another country. The cultural section of the relevant embassy or the tourist board will able to supply details on request of language courses taking place in a particular country, and useful addresses are given below. Usually such information will be sent in the form of a booklet listing courses, plus details of any grants available, so when writing it is wise to enclose a large stamped self-addressed envelope to be sure of a speedy reply.

The Central Bureau publishes **Study Holidays**, a guide for those wishing to study a language in the country in which it is spoken. It provides detailed informed on over 600 organisations offering European language courses in 25 countries. New edition published spring 1992 and available from all good bookshops or from the Central Bureau (£8.95 including postage).

Another way to improve language skills is to take part in a homestay, where you are welcomed into the home of a foreign family. This provides an excellent opportunity to immerse yourself completely in another lifestyle, language and culture. The Central Bureau's guidebook **Home From Home** gives details of agencies arranging homestays in many countries, plus full information on travel and preparation, and contacts for bed and breakfast accommodation and farmstays. Available from bookshops or £7.99 by post from the Central Bureau.

If you would rather study in this country there are organisations such as the Alliance Française or the Goethe-Institut, responsible for promoting their country's language and culture, who organise day and evening classes. Your local library will also be able to provide information on language courses available at nearby schools or colleges.

Danish
Cultural Section, Royal Danish Embassy, 55 Sloane Street, London SW1X 9SR ✆ 071-235 1255 can supply a list of Danish language courses.

Danish Cultural Institute, 3 Doune Terrace, Edinburgh EH3 6DY ✆ 031-225 7189 organises evening Danish language classes in cooperation with the universities of Edinburgh and Stirling.

Dutch
Cultural Section, Belgian Embassy, 103 Eaton Square, London SW1W 9AB ✆ 071-235 5422 publishes a leaflet *Dutch and French courses in Belgium* providing lists of courses organised by universities and language schools.

Cultural Section, Royal Netherlands Embassy, 38 Hyde Park Gate, London SW7 5DP ✆ 071-584 5040 publishes *Private Language Schools in the Netherlands,* a listing of intensive Dutch courses.

Finnish

Cultural Section, Finnish Embassy, 32 Grosvenor Gardens, London SW1W ODH ✆ 071-235 9531 can supply details of Finnish courses in Finland and in Britain.

French

Cultural Section, Belgian Embassy, 103 Eaton Square, London SW1W 9AB ✆ 071-235 5422 publishes a leaflet *Dutch and French courses in Belgium* providing lists of courses organised by universities and language schools.

Cultural Section, French Embassy, 22 Wilton Crescent, London SW1 ✆ 071-235 8080 can provide a booklet *Cours de Français pour Étudiants Étrangers* giving information on all types of courses in French as a foreign language. Available in two editions, one dealing with summer courses, the other covering courses available all year.

Alliance Française, 1 Dorset Square, London NW1 6PU ✆ 071-723 6439 runs language courses at all levels and for all ages. Alliance Française and French Chamber of Commerce examinations may be taken.

Institut Français, 14 Cromwell Place, London SW7 2JR ✆ 071-581 2701 is the official centre for French language and culture in London, depending directly on the French Ministry of Foreign Affairs. Offers courses in French for all levels and an extensive programme of cultural activities.

Swiss National Tourist Office, Swiss Centre, Swiss Court, London W1V 8EE ✆ 071-734 1921 issues *The Swiss Universities,* a guide to university education in Switzerland, and *Holidays and Language Courses,* an annual table of holiday opportunities available in Swiss private schools, state schools, holiday camps and universities.

German

Austrian Institute, 28 Rutland Gate, London SW7 1PQ ✆ 071-584 8653 is the cultural section of the Austrian Embassy; can provide information on grants for study in Austria.

Anglo-Austrian Society, 46 Queen's Gate, London SW1H 9AU ✆ 071-222 0366 is a charity promoting Anglo-Austrian relations. Acts as an agent for language courses, arranges exchange visits and runs intensive German courses at Christmas and Easter.

Cultural Section, German Embassy, 23 Belgrave Square, London SW1X 8PZ ✆ 071-235 5033 can supply details of language courses in Germany.

German Academic Exchange Service, 17 Bloomsbury Square, London WC1A 2LP ✆ 071-404 4065 can provide a list of language courses at German universities.

Goethe Institute, 50 Princes Gate, Exhibition Road, London SW7 2PG ✆ 071-581 3344
Goethe Institute, Ridgefield House, 14 John Dalton Square, Manchester M2 6JR ✆ 071-834 4635
Goethe Institute, The King's Manor, Exhibition Square, York YO1 2EP ✆ York (0904) 55222
Scottish-German Centre, Lower Medway Building, 74 Victoria Crescent Road, Glasgow G12 9SC ✆ 041-334 6116
A non-profitmaking organisation aimed at promoting German language and culture, with branches throughout Germany, in Britain and over 60 countries worldwide. Runs German courses, advises teachers of German and grants scholarships for the study of German.

Swiss National Tourist Office, *see above.*

Greek

Cultural Section, Greek Embassy, 1a Holland Park, London W11 3TP ✆ 071-727 8040 can provide information on language courses in Greece.

Italian
Italian Cultural Institute, 39 Belgrave Square, London SW1X 8NX © 071-235 1461 publishes *Italian Government Scholarships and Grants,* which gives details on how to apply for bursaries, grants and scholarships. Also publishes an annual booklet *Cultural and Language Courses in Italy,* and can provide current brochures on most courses listed.

Swiss National Tourist Office, *see above.*

Norwegian
Cultural Section, Royal Norwegian Embassy, 25 Belgrave Square, London SW1X 8QD © 071-235 7151 can provide details of language courses in Norway.

Portuguese
Portuguese National Tourist Office, New Bond Street House, 1-5 New Bond Street, London W1Y 9PE © 071-493 3873 can provide information on language courses in Portugal.

Calouste Gulbenkian Foundation, 98 Portland Place, London W1N 4ET © 071-636 5313 maintains cultural and educational centres in Portugal and offers grants for projects in the fields of arts, education, social welfare and Anglo-Portuguese relations.

Hispanic & Luso Brazilian Council, Canning House, 2 Belgrave Square, London SW1X 8PJ © 071-235 2303 gives information and advice on all matters relating to Portugal, Spain and Latin America, including language courses and travel. Organises lectures, runs cultural events and can advise on grants.

Spanish
Spanish Institute, 102 Eaton Square, London SW1W 9AN Tel 071-235 1484 arranges Spanish language courses and cultural events, and provides an information service. Holds consultation copies of *Cursos de Lengua y de Cultura para Extranjeros en España,* an annual booklet giving details of Spanish language courses available from the Servizio de Publicaciones, Ministerio de Educacion y

Ciencia, Ciudad Universitaria, 28040 Madrid, Spain.

Hispanic & Luso Brazilian Council, *see above.*

Swedish
Cultural Section, Swedish Embassy, 11 Montagu Place, London W1H 2AL © 071-724 2101 issues an annual publication *Svenska Institutets Internationalla Sommarkurser,* which gives information on summer courses organised by the *Svenska Institutet* in association with various Folk High Schools in Sweden.

The Grants Register 1991-1993 covers travel grants, exchange opportunities, vacation study awards as well as scholarships, fellowships and research grants and funding for many other projects. Published by Macmillan and usually available for reference in public libraries.

Term stays A term stay involves attending a foreign school for one or two terms or for a full academic year. There are some opportunities to attend boarding schools, but in most cases accommodation is in carefully selected host families, where the participant may be matched with a partner of the same age and interests. Term stays provide the opportunity to become totally immersed not just in family life, but in school and community life as well.

In general, term stay opportunities are open only to students who are still attending school, but the organisations listed on the following pages are able to cater for those wishing to attend a foreign school after leaving school in this country, as part of their year between. For those interested in a term stay in the United States however, it should be noted that one of the US visa requirements is that participants must be under 19 years old on 1 January of the year that they intend to take part in the term stay.

AMERICAN INSTITUTE FOR
FOREIGN STUDY

Kenneth Matthews, American Institute for Foreign Study, 16 Young Street, London W8 5EH

071-938 4944

United States

The American Institute for Foreign Study was founded in 1964 to provide study and travel programmes for teachers and students interested in learning about other cultures. The AIFS Scholarship Foundation was established in 1968 to promote international understanding through cross-cultural exchange.

Term stays are arranged throughout the United States. Students are placed in carefully selected families, attend school and take part in school and family activities.

Ages 15-18. Applicants must provide school reports for the last 3 years, 2 letters of recommendation from teachers and a health certificate.

5 or 10 months, beginning January or August

Cost $2,800 for 5 months, $3,600 for 10 months. Costs cover placement, accommodation, orientation, health and accident insurance. Students pay their own travel costs and incidental expenses such as pocket money and school lunch.

Staff meet students on arrival. 3-day orientation programme held in New York.

Apply by 1 October for January departure, by 1 April for August departure

CENTRAL BUREAU SCOTLAND

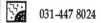

Central Bureau for Educational Visits & Exchanges, 3 Bruntsfield Crescent, Edinburgh EH10 4HD

031-447 8024

Germany: Bavaria, Schleswig-Holstein and Nordrhein-Westfalen

The Central Bureau for Educational Visits & Exchanges was set up in 1948 by the British government to act as the national office for the provision of information and advice on all forms of educational visits and exchanges. The Scottish office opened in 1972.

Arranges term stays in Germany where participants are placed with host families and attend a local school

Ages 16-18. Scottish applicants only; participants should be recommended by their schools and must have a good knowledge of German.

12-14 weeks, autumn or spring term

Details of full programme costs given on application. Participants pay for their own travel, which can be arranged independently or with the assistance of the Central Bureau.

Apply by end September for spring visits, end April for autumn visits

CLUB DE RELACIONES CULTURALES INTERNACIONALES

The President, Club de Relaciones Culturales Internacionales, Calle de Ferraz 82, 28008 Madrid, Spain

Madrid (1) 541 7103

All areas of Spain, except Catalonia

A non-profitmaking, cultural, educational and linguistic association offering a wide-ranging international programme for young people wishing to broaden their knowledge of foreign languages and cultures

Can place young people in state or private schools, with accommodation in family homes. The scheme operates on a reciprocal basis; families are usually required to accommodate a Spanish student in their home.

Ages 10-28. Applicants complete a detailed form to enable suitable matching of personal characteristics, family, school, extra-curricular activities, hobbies and special interests. Medical certificate and teacher's reference must be supplied. Knowledge of Spanish not essential, as Spanish tuition is included in regular school programme.

1 term-1 full academic year

Participants pay a £40 registration fee, plus travel and insurance costs. As this is a reciprocal scheme, no charge for accommodation or schooling is involved.

Apply all year round

ENGLISH-SPEAKING UNION OF THE COMMONWEALTH

The Director of Education, English-Speaking Union, Dartmouth House, 37 Charles Street, London W1X 8AB

071-493 3328

Canada and the United States

A registered charity founded in 1918 with the aim of promoting international understanding. Administers a wide variety of educational programmes including school scholarships to North America.

The object of the scholarships is to enable British school leavers to spend an additional year as senior students at schools in Canada and the United States. Placements are mainly at independent boarding schools in many parts of North America, the majority in the New England States.

Applicants should be British, have taken A levels (or equivalent) and not exceed the age of 19½ before they leave Britain. Their schools are asked to submit full confidential reports; a medical certificate is also required.

3 terms, beginning September, or 2 terms, beginning January

Students are provided with free board and lodging at the school. In the case of day schools, students stay with a host family, for which a weekly contribution is required. Hospitality may be provided during the shorter holidays; students are permitted to travel at the end of the academic year. Students pay their own travel expenses and insurance, plus a deposit of $300 each term to cover incidental expenses. Application fee £3, administration fee £50; refundable deposit £50. An entrance fee of £10 is also payable if the school is not a member of the ESU's School Affiliation Scheme.

Short-listed candidates must attend an interview at Dartmouth House

Apply by 1 February for September departure; by 1 October for January departure

EUROPEAN EDUCATIONAL OPPORTUNITIES PROGRAMME

The Director, European Educational Opportunities Programme, 28 Canterbury Road, Lydden, Dover, Kent CT15 7ER

Tel Dover (0304) 823631   Fax (0304) 825869

France, Germany, United States

A non-profitmaking organisation founded in 1986 aiming to offer homestay and term stay programmes through carefully selected homes, schools and allied agencies

Can place students in French, German and American schools, with accommodation in host families. Students are integrated totally into family life and enter fully into school academic and social programmes.

Ages 16+. Applicants must be recommended by their own school. Reasonable fluency in the language of the country selected is required.

1-3 terms

For French and German stays a fee from £440 per month is required to cover accommodation and placement. For the United States fees are £2,950 for 5 months, $3,650 for 10 months. Participants arrange their own travel and insurance.

Private language tuition can be arranged, if necessary

France and Germany: apply at least 1 month in advance; United States: apply at least 3 months in advance

INTERCULTURAL EDUCATIONAL PROGRAMMES

The Director, Intercultural Educational Programmes, Ground Floor Suite, Arden House, Main Street, Bingley, West Yorkshire

Bingley (0274) 560677

Many countries throughout North America, Latin America, Asia, Australasia and Europe; different countries are selected each year

A registered charity founded in 1947 as a partner of the American organisation AFS Intercultural Programs. Their aim is to work towards peace through international understanding by promoting new relationships in which people from different cultural backgrounds share new learning situations.

Participants attend a foreign school full-time and become a member of the local community. They are carefully placed in a family and community which complements their background.

Ages 16-18 (some destinations will accept 19 year olds). Applicants should be attending school at time of application, be in good health, and willing to give a lot to the experience. No special language knowledge required.

11 months beginning July/August or January/February. Participants may return early, especially if intending to return to higher education in September.

Cost from £700-£3,450 includes travel, placement in school and family, accommodation, insurance, medical expenses, orientation courses, group activities, and support and supervision throughout the stay. Parents are asked to make a realistic contribution within their means; participants will be encouraged to seek grants from local trusts and companies. Host families are volunteers and receive no money for hosting.

Cultural orientation courses organised; introductory language course provided on arrival where necessary

Apply before November of year prior to commencement of programme; late applicants occasionally considered

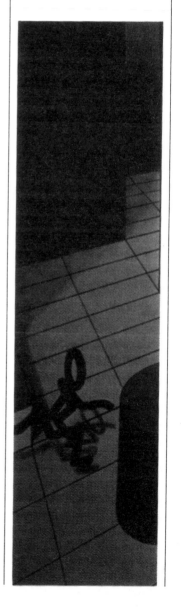

TRAVEL ADVICE

Some placement organisations are happy to make or advise on travel arrangements, although this service is not always included in the fee. Others expect individuals to make their own arrangements. There are a number of operators specialising in youth travel; details of some of them are given below. It is advisable to book only with those who are members of the Association of British Travel Agents (ABTA) or the International Association of Travel Agents (IATA), and to book flights only with agents who hold an Air Travel Organisers Licence (ATOL).

Eurolines, 23 Crawley Road, Luton LU1 1HX ✆ Luton (0582) 404511 offers a range of coach services to over 200 destinations in mainland Europe, including daily services to Paris, Amsterdam, Brussels, Frankfurt and Cologne.

The British Rail International Rail Centre, Victoria Station, London SW1V 1JY ✆ 071-928 5151 can issue those under 26 with Euro-Youth low cost rail tickets to any one of 200 selected destinations in mainland Europe. Also issues Inter-Rail passes providing up to 1 month's unlimited travel on the railways of 24 countries in Europe and around the Mediterranean; available both to those under 26 and ages 26+. European timetables and assistance with journey planning available.

Campus Travel, 52 Grosvenor Gardens, London SW1W 0AG ✆ 071-730 3402 (offices throughout the UK) and Council Travel, 28A Poland Street, London W1V 3DB ✆ 071-437 7767 offer Eurotrain under 26 fares to many destinations in Europe and low cost student/ youth airfares to destinations worldwide.

STA Travel, 74 Old Brompton Road, London SW7 3LQ ✆ 071-937 9962 (offices also in Birmingham, Bristol, Cambridge, Leeds, Manchester and Oxford) operates flexible, low-cost flights worldwide.

Trailfinders Travel Centre, 42-50 Earls Court Road, London W8 6EJ ✆ 071-938 3366 and Trailfinders, 194 Kensington High Street, London W8 7RG ✆ 071-938 3939 operate low-cost flights between London and destinations worldwide. Also have a travellers' library, bookshop and information centre, and an immunization centre for travel vaccinations.

North-South Travel, Moulsham Mill, Parkway, Chelmsford, Essex CM2 7PX ✆ Chelmsford (0245) 492882 arranges competitively prices, reliably planned flights to many destinations. Profits are paid into a trust fund for the assignment of aid to projects in the poorest areas of the South.

Customs Details of UK Customs regulations are given in *Notice 1: The Customs Allowances* available from HM Customs & Excise or from Customs at ports and airports in the UK. There are prohibitions and restrictions on the importation of certain goods ranging from drugs and weapons to foodstuffs and plants. Further information from local enquiry offices or from HM Customs & Excise, General Information Branch, Dorset House, Stamford Street, London SE1 9PS ✆ 071-620 1313.

Money The amount of money you require will depend on a variety of factors, including the services already covered in any fee levied, the cost of living in the country you will be visiting, and the total length of time you will be away, including what proportion of this period will be spent travelling rather than on placement. The placement organisation should be able to advise on how much money to take to cover expenses. If you are going to be in paid employment you will need some money to live on until your first pay day; this need only be pocket money if food and accommodation are being found for you. On the other hand, you may have to pay for your board, lodging and other needs, and you may be paid monthly, not weekly. If you're undertaking voluntary work in a remote location, with food and accommodation provided, pocket money may be enough to cover your needs, and you may even find difficulty in finding somewhere to spend it! It is advisable for any visitor to a foreign country to have sufficient funds, preferably in travellers' cheques, to cover unforeseen circumstances. A good guide is to ensure enough is taken to pay for one or two nights' hotel accommodation and a long-distance telephone call. If you do run out of funds it is possible to arrange for money to be transferred to a bank abroad.

Large amounts of money are best taken as travellers' cheques; when obtaining these from a bank or travel agency you'll generally need to give a few days' notice and produce your passport. Shop around beforehand to compare commission rates charged. Some travellers' cheques can be replaced while you are still abroad, others will be honoured by the issuing bank on your return. If you are visiting North or South America, US$ travellers' cheques can be used as cash. If you have a current account you will probably be able to obtain a supply of Eurocheques and a cheque card. These can be cashed at most European banks and in many cases are accepted by shops and restaurants. You'll also need to carry some local currency; you can get this at major travel agents and banks. Again, shop around for the best exchange and commission rates. Don't forget to take some of your own currency with you for use on the outward and return journeys.

Passports A UK passport costs £15 and is valid for 10 years. A 94 page passport, useful for those intending to travel through many countries, is available at a cost of £30. Both are obtainable from regional offices:

Passport Office, Clive House, 70-78 Petty France, London SW1H 9HD ℡ 071-279 3434

Passport Office, 5th Floor, India Buildings, Water Street, Liverpool L2 0QZ ℡ 051-237 3010

Passport Office, Olympia House, Upper Dock Street, Newport, Gwent NP9 1XA ℡ Newport (0633) 244500

Passport Office, Aragon Court, Northminster Road, Peterborough, Cambridgeshire PE1 1QG ℡ Peterborough (0733) 895555

Passport Office, 3 Northgate, 96 Milton Street, Cowcaddens, Glasgow G4 0BT ℡ 041-332 0271

Passport Office, Hampton House, 47-53 High Street, Belfast BT1 2QS ℡ Belfast (0232) 232371

Application forms are available at main post offices. The completed form should be sent or taken to the regional passport office. Processing the application takes at least four weeks, and can take even longer during the summer months. Within western Europe and certain other specified countries, British citizens can travel on a British Visitor's Passport (BVP). This costs £7.50 and is valid for 12 months. Application forms are available from any main post office and should be returned there; in most cases the BVP will be issued immediately. Applicants from Northern Ireland, Jersey, Guernsey and the Isle of Man must obtain them from their area passport office. The BVP can be issued to British citizens, British Dependent Territories citizens and British Overseas citizens for holiday purposes of up to 3 months. *Essential information for holders of UK passports who intend to travel overseas* contains notes on illness or injury while abroad, insurance, vaccinations, consular assistance overseas, British Customs and other useful advice, and is available from all passport offices. If a passport is lost or stolen while abroad, the local police should be notified immediately; if necessary the nearest British embassy or consulate will issue a substitute. It is wise to keep a separate note of your passport number.

Visas For entry into some countries a visa or visitor's pass is required, and in many countries a residence permit will be required. Organisations arranging placements in such countries will be able to advise, and details of application procedures are available from the consular section of the relevant embassy. Regulations are subject to change without warning, and you are advised to obtain precise information before setting out.

Identity cards The International Student Identity Card (ISIC) gives internationally accepted proof of student status and consequently ensures that card holders may enjoy many special facilities including fare reductions, cheap accommodation, reduced rates or free entry to museums, art galleries and historical sites. The card is available to all full-time students, price £5, along with the *International Student Travel Guide* detailing the discounts and facilities available. Those taking a year between will not be classified as full-time students, but the card is valid for up to 16 months (1 September-31 December of following year) and is still valid after student status has ceased. Details in the UK from ISIC Administration, NUS Services Ltd, Bleaklow House, Howard Town Mills, Glossop SK13 8PT ℂ Glossop (0457) 868003.

The Federation of International Youth Travel Organisations (FIYTO) aims to promote educational, cultural and social travel amongst young people. The FIYTO International Youth Card is a recognised card offering concessions including transport, accommodation, restaurants, excursions, cultural events and reduced rates or free entry to many museums and art galleries. The card costs £4 and is valid for one year from date of issue. Available to those aged 12-26, together with a booklet giving details of concessions. Details in the UK from Campus Travel offices (London office: 52 Grosvenor Gardens, London SW1W 0AG ℂ 071-730 3402).

European Youth Cards are concessionary cards issued by a number of agencies, entitling holders to a range of discounts and special offers on travel, cultural events and goods in shops in 15 European countries. Cards are renewable annually, and holders receive a directory and a regular magazine of new discounts and activities available.
England and Wales: Under 26 Card available from the National Youth Agency, 17-23 Albion Street, Leicester LE1 6GD ℂ Leicester (0533) 471200, cost £6.
Scotland: Young Scot Card available from the Scottish Community Education Council, West Coates House, 90 Haymarket Terrace, Edinburgh EH12 5LQ ℂ 031-313 2433, cost £6.
Northern Ireland and Ireland: European Youth Card available from USIT, Fountain Centre, Belfast BT1 6ET ℂ Belfast (0232) 324073/USIT, Aston Quay, O'Connell Bridge, Dublin 2 ℂ Dublin (1) 778117, and other USIT offices, cost £5/IR£5.

Health Changes in food and climate may cause minor illnesses, and, especially when visiting the hotter countries of southern Europe, North Africa, Latin America and the Far East it is wise to take extra care in your hygiene, eating and drinking habits. Native bacteria, to which local inhabitants are immune, may cause the visitor stomach upsets, so it is worth avoiding tap water and doing without ice in your drinks. In a hot climate never underestimate the strength of the sun, nor overestimate your own strength. Drink plenty of fluid, make sure there is enough salt in your diet, wear loose-fitting cotton clothes, even a hat, and guard against heat exhaustion, heat stroke and sunburn.
In the UK the Department of Health issues two leaflets T2 *Health Advice for Travellers Inside the European Community*, available from post offices, and T3 *Health Advice for Travellers Outside the European Community*, available from travel agents, libraries and doctors' surgeries. These include details of compulsory and recommended vaccinations, other measures that can be taken to protect one's health, information on yellow fever, cholera, hepatitis, typhoid, tetanus, polio, malaria, rabies and AIDS, and action to take in an emergency. There is also advice on types of food and on water supplies which may be a source of infection. A certificate of vaccination against certain diseases is an entry requirement for some countries. The

organisation arranging your placement should be able to advise you; or consult the relevant embassy, as requirements are continually subject to review. A general recommendation is to make sure that your protection against typhoid, polio and tetanus is up-to-date if you are travelling outside Europe, North America or Australasia. Up-to-the-minute information on recommended immunizations and precautions to take against food poisoning is available from the Medical Advisory Service to Travellers Abroad (MASTA), London School of Hygiene and Tropical Medicine, Keppel Street, London WC1E 7HT © 071-631 4408. British Airways also run travel clinics throughout Britain; for details of the nearest one © 071-831 5333. Protection against some diseases takes the form of a course of injections over several weeks, so allow plenty of time.

Whilst abroad it is unwise to have your skin pierced by acupuncture, tattooing or ear piercing, for example, unless you can be sure that the equipment is sterile. A major cause of the spread of viruses, including AIDS, is the use of infected needles and equipment. In some countries blood for transfusions is not screened for the presence of the AIDS virus, but there may be arrangements for obtaining screened blood. The doctor treating you, or the nearest British consulate or embassy may be able to offer advice. If you are concerned about the availability of sterile equipment whilst abroad, emergency travel kits are available through MASTA, see above, and other suppliers, and can be ordered through retail pharmacists. They contain a variety of sterilised and sealed items such as syringes and needles for use in emergencies.

If you are taking prescribed drugs it is advisable to carry a doctor's letter giving details of the medical condition and the medication, avoiding the possibility of confusion. It will also be useful to find out the generic rather than the brand name of the medicine, so that if need arises further supplies can be obtained abroad.

Reciprocal health agreements A person is only covered by the NHS while in the UK, and will usually have to pay the full costs of any treatment abroad. However, there are health care agreements between all EC countries (Belgium, Britain, Denmark, France, Germany, Greece, Ireland, Italy, Luxembourg, the Netherlands, Portugal and Spain). British citizens resident in the UK will receive free or reduced cost emergency treatment in other EC countries on production of form E111 (available from post offices). Leaflet T2, see above, explains who is covered by the arrangements, what treatment is free or at reduced cost, and gives the procedures which must be followed to get treatment in countries where form E111 is not needed (usually Denmark, Ireland and Portugal). Form E111 is issued with information on how to get emergency medical treatment in other EC countries. Form E111 or leaflet T2 must be taken abroad and, if treatment is needed, the correct procedures must be followed.

There are also reciprocal health care agreements between Britain and Australia, Austria, Bulgaria, Channel Islands, Czechoslovakia, Finland, Gibraltar, Hong Kong, Hungary, Iceland, Isle of Man, Malta, New Zealand, Norway, Poland, Romania, Sweden, USSR, Yugoslavia and the British Dependent Territories of Anguilla, British Virgin Islands, Falkland Islands, Montserrat, St Helena, and Turks and Caicos Islands. However, private health insurance may still be needed in these countries; leaflet T3 (mentioned above) should be read to check the services available. Despite reciprocal health arrangements it is **essential** to take out full medical insurance when travelling overseas. The health treatment available in other countries may not be as comprehensive as in the UK, and **none** of the arrangements cover the cost of repatriation in the event of illness.

Social security Not all volunteer agencies pay national insurance contributions on behalf of participants, and you are well-advised to obtain beforehand details of your social security rights. The UK has reciprocal agreements with Australia, Austria, Bermuda, Canada, Cyprus, Finland, Iceland, Isle of Man, Israel, Jamaica, Jersey and Guernsey, Malta, Mauritius, New Zealand, Norway, Philippines, Sweden, Switzerland, Turkey, United States and Yugoslavia. Leaflets explaining these agreements and how they affect UK nationals are available from the Newcastle Benefits Directorate, *see below*.

Leaflet *SA29 Your Social Security and Pension Rights in the European Community* gives details of the social security rights available to UK nationals working in the EC and how to claim them. Separate booklets describe the social security schemes (including health services) available in certain EC countries. Leaflet *NI38 Social Security Abroad* is a guide to National Insurance contributions and social security benefits in non-EC and non-reciprocal agreement countries. For copies of these leaflets and any further information contact the Newcastle Benefits Office, Overseas Branch, Longbenton, Newcastle Upon Tyne NE98 1YX ✆ 091-225 3002.

Insurance Many organisations arranging placements either include insurance cover in the placement fee or can arrange it at additional cost. It is important to ascertain exactly what is included in the cover offered, as frequently it is limited to third party risk and accidents It is up to you to decide exactly what extent of insurance cover you require, but typical cover should include cancellation and delay, medical and emergency travel expenses, personal accident, loss of luggage and money, and personal liability.
The International Student Insurance Service (ISIS) policy is a leading policy for young travellers and provides, at competitive rates, a wide range of benefits covering death, disablement, medical and other personal expenses, loss of luggage, personal liability and cancellation, loss of deposits or curtailment. An advantage of this policy is that medical expenses can be settled on the spot in many countries; the medical limit for

these expenses relates to each claim and therefore the cover is, in effect, limitless. A 24-hour assistance service is provided to handle medical emergencies. Details in the UK from local Endsleigh Insurance centres.

Problems The organisation arranging your placement must be your first contact should any problems arise. However, if any dire emergency occurs whilst you are travelling independently you should contact the British Consul. There are consular offices at British embassies in foreign capitals and at consulates in some provincial cities. Consuls maintain a list of English-speaking doctors and will advise or help in case of serious difficulty or distress. As a last resort a consul can arrange for a direct return to the UK by the cheapest possible passage, providing the person concerned agrees to have their passport withdrawn and gives written agreement that they will pay the travel expenses involved. If the consul's urgent help is needed you should telephone or telegraph. The telegraphic address of all British Embassies is *Prodrome* and of all British Consulates *Britain*, followed in each case by the name of the appropriate town.

If you lose your ticket at the last minute, you should contact the airline/shipping company immediately to see if a replacement can be issued. If luggage is lost during a flight, the duty officer of the airline concerned should be informed immediately. If the luggage cannot be traced, a claim form must be completed. Most airlines will immediately provide a small payment to cover necessities, but they are under no obligation to do so, and the amount varies considerably from airline to airline. If after 3-4 weeks the luggage still has not been found, compensation will be paid by the airline according to the declaration made on the claim form. In any event, and to cover loss on other means of transport, it is advisable to take out a personal insurance policy which covers luggage loss. Any losses should of course be reported to the insurance company concerned.

INDEX

REPORT FORM

Up-to-date reports enable us to improve the accuracy and standard of information in our guidebooks, and monitor the opportunities available. Your completion and return of this form to the Print, Marketing and IT Unit, Central Bureau for Educational Visits and Exchanges, Seymour Mews House, Seymour Mews, London W1H 9PE, would therefore be much appreciated. **All reports will be treated in strict confidence**.

Name and address of organisation

How efficient were they in arranging the placement?

Type of placement

Where were you placed?

How long did the placement last?

Salary/terms of employment (where applicable)

PLEASE TURN OVER

Do you consider the fee you paid (if any) was justifiable?

Food and accommodation provided?

Age group of any other participants

Nationality of any other participants

Were your expectations achieved?

In what way do you think the experience was beneficial?

Name

Address

Age   Signed   Date